The Border: Immigration and the B.O.P

To order additional copies, please contact us.
BookSurge, LLC
www.booksurge.com
1-866-308-6235
orders@booksurge.com

The Border: Immigration and the B.O.P

Richard Alevizos

2006

The Border: Immigration and the B.O.P

INTRODUCTION

When I started to write this book and told some people they said; "Who cares about your life anyway? Do you think people care about criminals?" I was shocked. These were my family and friends saying this. So I resigned myself to write the book anyway.

Everyone has a story, its just boils down to if they know how to tell it. I hope I have told this small story interestingly enough to reach out to others and instigate some thought about where we are headed in this world.

When I first went to prison I looked at it as a very negative thing. Little by little I realized how lucky I was to be put in my situation because very few men or women are capable and desirous of writing about prison. There are so many men and women in prison who want desperately for their story to be told, but so few who do. So many times did I hear a man say; 'When I get out I am going to write a book about this." The reality of their situation is so far removed from what they thought would happen to them when they got out. To find the time required and inspiration needed to write a book is a hard thing to do after you have met your probation requirements for the day. It took me a year after I was released, and my probation requirements were pretty minimal. This book is for all the people whose stories never got out.

Someone once told me you can place a value on a thing only after its been through the worst of situations. Extrapolate that for a moment. For "thing" substitute any word. Person, country, president, senator, dog, parent, sibling, friend, car, government, prison system, border patrol, laws, sentencing guidelines. But wait, I'm getting a little personal and specific. Certainly a general situation like Hurricane Katrina tested the value of many of those "things" and the country at large. What happened certainly was tragic. The government's reaction time was just as tragic as the hurricane itself. We don't even know if their efforts will help in the long run. The nightmare stories coming out of New Orleans about what happened during the hurricane are just so tragic. Mentally disabled men being shot in the back and doctors killing patients in the hospital because they didn't think they were going to be able to move them.

How about the Tsunami in Indonesia? That put everyone in the world to the test. The sheer size of the destruction; 290,000 dead or missing (and missing at this point means also dead). Millions displaced with livelihoods and lives permanently damaged. What was our response? As a nation we sent the military in as a force for "humanitarian aide." It was a tremendous effort on the part of all, but it seemed like we were trying to compete with Europe and other countries as if to prove to the world who was truly the best. I think to this day there is far too much work left undone there. Work left undone because more than likely, much like the Katrina aide in this country, was squandered on fruitless no-bid contracts awarded to who knows who. Some of the aide that reached Indonesia was stolen and misspent by a few corrupt individuals. Who knows how much that might have been.

So how do we rectify that kind of corruption? Especially when the numbers are so large. The number of people involved and the number of tangible things that the money represents are hard to keep a track of. Things like tractors and other earth moving equipment, food aide, medical aide and other types of resources needed to help communities after natural disasters. How do you keep a track of all of it? To add to the problem there is no one who is truly keeping track of all of the money. In some instances there isn't even a committee of people to monitor how the money is spent to ensure the proper function of disaster aide.

There is another situation just as tragic as Katrina and the Indonesian Tsunami and it happens daily at our nations borders. If you take all that was just said about natural disasters and apply it to the border and the prison system it starts sounding even scarier. The border and the prison system are inextricably linked. The Bureau of Prisons' unquenchable thirst for federal tax dollars and the border's sheer size command a huge chunk of tax dollars. These tax dollars and the way they are used by the government on its borders and in its prison system can only be described as at once gargantuan and draconian. The number of people caught trying to cross the border in some illegal capacity every year is just so huge that the prison system couldn't possibly take them all. The number is so large the judicial system couldn't possibly process all the cases. It just wouldn't have the time and resources. There would be so many mistrials just for a lack of a timely trial by jury. Just a fraction is all that is needed to keep the judiciary at maximum capacity, and a relatively small fraction considering all the people detained at the border for trying to enter illegally who are time and time again being released without charges filed against them. The numbers of people caught crossing does not match the number of prosecutions there are and the number of people convicted of border crimes. I'd say what ever the numbers are they represent two things; one, the need to maintain quotas for budget projections so the amount of federal tax dollars doesn't decrease for the agencies involved, namely the Bureau of Prisons, the judiciary; the courts, prosecutors and public defenders offices, and the Border Patrol. The Border Patrol actually is only part of what protects the border so when we are talking about money to be spent on protecting the border we are talking about the Coast Guard, Customs and Immigration and the Border Patrol. Each have separate budgets under the new agency created to manage them all (just what we needed was another layer of bureaucracy to waste our money); Homeland Security. We can thank George Bush for this mega agency which tends to waste more money than ever before even though it was supposed to save money. Homeland Security is our new modern day Gestapo. Hitler's own creation. And who said fascism was dead? So when you see these jeeps that say "Federal Protective Service" you know that that vehicle belongs to Homeland security.

It is just a federal feast on the tax payers' money instigated and orchestrated by the Bush family and its cronies. There was no need for another layer of government, i.e. Homeland Security. There was no need for a war in Iraq. And there is little need for a prison and criminal justice complex such as ours either. But the avarice and the greed of the Bushes and their buddies has created a country where we are less free and our country's money is being used for their own personal agenda. That would be my wild guess at it. Their personal agenda is not good for you and me. The judicial had to be in on this federal feast of the taxpayers money by being cajoled along by the Attorney Generals of the last 20 years to allow trials for all kinds of things, but just enough and not to much so as not to overburden the courts. With the judicial branch's part, we have a veritable triumvirate of power thirsting for more federal tax dollars and all grinding together in sync to a rhythm out of touch with the people and out of touch with a changing global economy.   Remember, of the past 26 years we had a democratic president for only eight of them. The rest of the time it was those wonderful Republicans who lead this country down a road of arrogant selfish egotism based on supposed Christian self righteousness. Combined with a national foreign policy of seeking dominion over other countries, and when we can't, instigating "regime change" to achieve our corporate goals abroad, it is our government's internal domestic policy towards its own people which constitute the very fascism we supposedly fought against in WWII.

Today the problems the border present are so manifold and widespread that for a lawmaker to say its as easy as putting up a fence is ludicrous. Or to send the National Guard. Or to say lets just make them all felons if they try it, is also ridiculous. Some say Mexico should take better care of its people. Its true. Where is the middle class in Mexico today? There isn't one. But its not just Mexico's fault. Its either ultra rich or mega poor. If you're ultra rich its easy for you to get a temporary tourist visa because our country doesn't have to worry about you overstaying your welcome because your rich and your power base is in Mexico. If you are poor you don't stand a snowball's chance in hell of ever getting a visa to come in. Certain people who live on the border can get these work visas to do service industry jobs in places like San Diego, El Paso, Brownsville etc. But only at the border and only for those jobs they indicated. There are all kinds of restrictions about these kinds of work visas too, like you can't go more than so many miles into the country. But these visas and visa holders aren't the problem. The problem isn't all entirely because there is no middle class in Mexico, far from it.   Some say NAFTA was supposed to help Mexico with their middle class problem. But NAFTA didn't do that. Not even close. Its true a lot of companies went south of the border. Just south. Most of the factories built in Mexico by U.S. companies lie just south of the border in border towns or in northern states in Mexico. These factories moved south because of cheaper labor and less environmental restrictions. Because the intent was to take advantage of cheap labor, the jobs created were never intended to create a middle class in Mexico.

NAFTA in general was a bad deal for Mexico's people. It was also a bad deal for average Americans this side of the border. The factory closings in the U.S. in the 90's and to date may have been good news to U.S. corporations, but it wasn't good news to the U.S. worker.

NAFTA and the lack of a Mexican middle class aren't solely to blame for the problem at the border. So if its not Mexico's fault for not creating a middle class by offering better paying jobs, and its not NAFTA's fault then what? Some will say this "problem" at the border is about drug illegality, about poverty, about power and how it is used to take advantage of people who were down and out on their luck. People who felt like they had no other option in life but to commit a crime. This book is about the very society at large that permits things to happen without so much as even a yawn instead of standing up against the erosion of its very rights and civil liberties. NAFTA and the notion that Mexico should be more responsible for its own people are background events to a situation that has taken the forefront without any reason for it other than its own self perpetuating idea that we need the criminal justice system and prison system.

People try to cross to the Land of Opportunity only to be shackled and stuffed into a prison. What is wrong with them? Why only some people? Some of them come to work in the fields to provide food for the people of this land or other jobs just as basic and low paying. Somehow a seemingly arbitrary system has been put in place to determine which ones are not worth anything to us. This supposed system determines whether they as humans, are illegal or legal.

The story you are about to read is one man's relatively brief encounter with one of the ugliest dirty little secrets this country doesn't want you to know about. Immigration. At least, not in any real way that might make you question how the government is handling it. What little that does get discussed in the media is always geared towards what the potential economic impact of crossing the borders is. The links between the Federal Bureau of Prisons, the Border and the judiciary is what I have commonly come to refer to as the Holy Judicial Juggernaut, the spearhead of which is the Southern District of California. San Diego and the 9th Circuit Court in particular and the border in general. More cases are tried there and along the border than anywhere else in the whole country. Understandably the amount of Federal dollars spent there has to be enormous and larger than anywhere else in the federal Judicial bureaucracy. Millions of dollars which is spent on prosecuting and incarcerating our low wage work force and our country's most destitute poor and homeless. Are we helping anyone? Or is our country caught in a cycle of judicial nonsense which can only be described as new age fascism?

This is why I am writing this. I am like so many Americans living under the federal government's poverty level. When I have been in need my government wasn't there for me. The rich will tell you not to need anyone. But this is wrong. We all need each other in even the most indirect of ways. Just the simple act of buying a loaf of bread sets up a whole chain reaction of togetherness without which people would go without bread. The farmer to make the wheat, Someone to thresh it, transport it, mill it into flour, send it to the bakery. Bake it. Transport it again to the store. And finally sell it to you. So we all need each other. Everybody has a vital role to play in this life.

I have a college education. I am outraged and my voice is my only weapon. A voice many others don't have because they are simply not literate enough to explain what happened to them. Or its not that they can't read and write, they just don't speak English. This is a book of stories, of voices you will never hear. They have been silenced or they were never allowed to be voiced to begin with. All the stories are different but they are one and the same. They all reflect the multifaceted problem which the border represents.

People suffering, living without all their basic needs are eventually going to be forced to perform desperate acts to ensure their own survival. This is just a basic instinct of any living life form on this planet. For poverty stricken people living in Mexico, before it is anything else, crossing the border for the better life our country prides itself on is a simple act of self-preservation.

It is only natural that in the interest of protecting its border our government is trying to keep them out. But we have created some seemingly arbitrary idea that some are okay and some are not. It is not so arbitrary as we would like to believe. Yet, more than we can imagine, we need the people we are building fences to keep out.

I crossed the border as one of my country's destitute and my story brings in another piece to this border puzzle. We are forgetting our duties as human beings. We are allowing people to become so hurt in our society, so lost that they believe they have no one to help them and thus they commit a crime. That was me and this is my story. These are the stories of people being kept in prison for no good reason, unnecessarily keeping millions of dollars wrapped up. Millions of dollars needed for other things like healthcare and education but are instead spent on prosecuting and convicting people for wanting a better life and being willing to do anything, anything no matter how dangerous, even if it meant to cross the border lying on top of an engine of a car. Just so she could get to L.A. to find a job mopping somebody else's floor for eight dollars an hour.

These are stories of people willing to never see their families just to make sure they can eat and have all they need. These are also the stories of the men that have been forgotten by the United States. This isn't a story of terrorists because the terrorists are the ones so frightened by themselves. They can no longer pin their title to anyone. Step into the fight on the borders and you will see. Those that talk of needing to catch and incarcerate the bad guys are more often than not talking of themselves. The voices never heard of are the vast majority and we are the ones getting screwed. The trouble with the Mexican border could be the chance for the people of both countries to rise up, get together and finally get their governments to resolve the problem once and for all. After all, anything is possible.

The issues with the border with Mexico should be constant reminders of racial discrimination. Illegal Mexican labor has replaced and displaced many black workers over the decades. My guess is that it is preferable to have an illegal alien because they can't speak English and can't rebel against any injustice. If he tried he would just lose his job and be thrown out of the country. Employers enjoy having so much control over their worker why would they hire a black or white man when he can hire somebody for two or three dollars lower and get a hard worker who won't complain? If we can look at the ramifications to what the government is doing by shutting out some people and letting others in we can begin to see it represents some significant life lessons for all of us.

Who is trying to get in the country through the Mexican Border? What are they trying to bring in? What are they trying to do when they get here? Whoever they are they really have an easy time of it, for the most part. After all, counting just the illegal Mexican population in the United States there are around 8 to ten million here illegally. So who's getting caught? Stragglers, sick or out of shape. Mother's with children. Or just simply the unlucky. You never hear of the top gangsters getting caught crossing the border. They don't need or want to. Terrorists? You'd have to be delusional to believe that a Taliban or al-Qaeda terrorist would try to enter the country through San Diego or Texas. The strong and determined who don't get caught are the other 8 million who are right this minute working here to provide you with goods and services you desire to get on the cheap. Their labor allows them to send home badly needed money so that their families can simply get by and eek out a meager existence compared to families in our country.

You are about to discover why all the right wingers have no reason to be screaming bloody murder. The few "bad apples" that could be found in any society and the willing workers of the countries of Latin America are our governments scapegoats. Why are we allowing this? Are we not outraged that we are spending millions of dollars on keeping people out instead of focusing on our children's education and health?

With these stories we can see why our elected officials in the capitol are vying and jockeying themselves into position on this issue. And why, due to their personal and secret agendas they will do nothing about it except make it an election year issue like the ban on gay marriage to take our minds off of all the other bad things the federal government is doing. These stories will help you see them for who they really are, if you haven't already figured them out.

The only reason the Border exists today can be boiled down to one word; money. They call it "pork" on the hill. They call it "lana" or wool in Spanish. And just like its effect on everything else about our country and government, money is the number one problem that exists today which affects the border and border politics. The border represents trade. Tariffs and taxes are collected there from legitimate businesses. Bribes are collected to let illicit goods get through too. Just think, the money the government spends on prisons for people convicted at the border probably accounts for half of all federal prison dollars spent. Throw in court costs for judges, bailiffs, court reporters, federal security officers to staff federal courthouses, Federal Marshals to transport inmates to and from trial, prosecutors and public defenders and all their secretaries and private investigators and the courthouses themselves which I heard are quite spendy these days. Throw in all these things and the cost surges and mounts daily into a disgusting and unneeded expenditure of the tax payers' dollars. The government gets this money not only from the tax payers but also from the inmates and their families in the way of fines, property seizures and money collected once they are in prison. An additional financial burden that poor families don't need to shoulder. Money ruthlessly collected by the courts and foolishly spent by the government on who knows what. Money that hurts countless millions of people every day across the world. Rich and poor alike. If you ask the General Accounting Office they'll tell you one figure or another based on this or that statistical survey. The bottom line is, no matter what the figure is, it is all a waste and completely unnecessary. The border is just another artificial construct among many which have been designed to help the rich get richer and the poor get poorer. This is the story of the poor , the illegal and the forgotten. The generations of disenfranchised youth in our country who become street people or "couch surfers". People left behind by society, government and corporation alike.

At first when I got busted I had visions of wanting to tell my judge the whole story of my life and how I viewed the situation of the borders in the hopes he would prove to be one of those compassionate conservatives, but my attorney told me not to because as he said "don't ever try to remind the conservatives of that compassion part, they hate to be reminded of it and end up throwing the book at you for it. And the longer you speak the time is being wasted, he has other things to do." In no time at all they threw the book at me anyway simply for who I am.

In my mind there are two types of basic crimes. The crimes of need and the crimes of greed. I had committed a crime out of need. Kenneth Lay, the Enron exec, committed a crime purely out of greed. He didn't need more money. He didn't lack for anything. He was sitting in his multi-million dollar home or yacht scheming a way how to bilk billions of dollars out of the pockets of millions of people. And there are many others like him, selfishly and greedily scheming ways to connive us out of our little bits of money.

What had I done? I had tried to bring a Mexican lady across the border to provide for my family. The impact of the two crimes is vastly different. Kenny baby's crime impacted a whole nation, my crime just impacted myself and my family (because they suffered when I went to prison.)

The Mexican woman I drove across was an economic slave seeking freedom. She made the decision to put herself in a dangerous situation so she could be with her husband and hopefully create a better life for herself. She had deliberately draped herself over the lowered engine of a Plymouth Caravan so she could cross the border undetected. She called herself La Valienta. "The Valiant." And she was too. With only a heat retardant blanket over the engine and her on top we tried to cross the border. And failed.

The border between San Diego and Tijuana is the most heavily trafficked border in the world. Just by volume alone it makes it the most difficult border crossing to maintain security for. New sophisticated cameras have been placed there to sense everything from drugs to the heat of a human body. I'd like to call it a spectrograph gun or something. So factor in new sophisticated technology for the border into your incidental costs and the cost goes up even more. Mostly just to catch the little guy whose impact on society as a whole was nil when compared to the big guy like Kenneth Lay, who adversely impacted the lives of how many? And to the tune of how many billions?

But Valienta and me? We were committing crimes out of need for a better life. Although the judge and prosecutor would have you believe that the American people were the victim of my crime, I couldn't share that opinion with the judge. To him I am just a criminal and she is just an illegal. I crossed the border with another human being on top of the motor of a moving car. We were both simply trying to find a way to better our lives. In different ways we struggled to survive and the judge would never understand. So I must enter into the Land of Oz. Prison is cool you know, MTV has a show about it. Welcome to San Diego. Welcome to the reality of the US prison system.

THE BORDER: IMMIGRATION AND THE B.O.P

***

It was quiet on Range 8. I was on the seventh floor of MCC, the pre-trial unit. MCC, the Metropolitan Correction Center, was 20 stories tall or something like that. It is the main federal detention center for pre-trial inmates stuck inside because they could not make bail or did not have bail. The building towers over the federal courthouse across the street from it. A case could be made that the sole existence for downtown San Diego was these two buildings in the first place. Around them are all kinds of bail bondsmen's offices and nice restaurants and a mall that thrived only because of Legal activity there in the first place. Because five blocks uptown and it is teriyaki by the stick for a buck and countless strange street people that you just knew were not a part of the thriving downtown legal economic boom. Maybe they were victims of it.

A greyhound station and the bank also surround these two buildings. But MCC itself was a citadel of slitted concrete towering above it all.

It was slightly confusing because for most of the building, with the lower and upper floors being the exception, two normal floors combined to make one large floor with an upstairs and a downstairs. The seventh floor was a general population floor with 200 people split up into 8 "Ranges", or "ranchos" in Spanish. Each range had anywhere between 25 to 32 men depending on who was coming and going to and from trial. The original design concept back in the '70's called for each range holding only eight inmates per range. This is the perfect example of prison overcrowding; 32 in the space of what was intended for eight. It repeats itself across the prison system all the way into solitary confinement, which isn't so solitary anymore, and the government uses this overcrowding issue as its poor excuse why it needs to build more and more prisons instead of simply changing its approach to crime and punishment. But anything to fruitlessly spend money in the wrong direction. That was exactly where MCC has headed since 1988 or so.

The 7th floor was for all pretrial prisoners. When you arrived there as a new inmate you were given the top bunk of a bunk bed and maybe a locker if one was available. If you had a medical condition (that you could prove to a prison doctor) which prevented you from climbing into a top bunk then you were given a lower bunk. In most cases old age was not considered enough to give you a lower bunk. But inmates worked together on that and if an old guy came in with no medical problems to warrant a lower bunk somebody gave up their lower bunk that didn't really need it so that the senior citizen could have it . And this went across racial lines too. Prisoners will collaborate and bend over backwards to help the elderly. You could end up stuck on the seventh floor of MCC for two years waiting for your trial. Never moved once. You could go stir crazy up there and you haven't even gone to trial yet. What if you are innocent? While most men see the inside of prison for at least a day while they are waiting for bail, there are guys like San Diego City Councilmen who never took a step inside the prison system when they were "arrested" or "indicted" for their crimes. Guys like Kenneth Lay get to stay out on bail even after they've been found guilty when most post conviction inmates are behind bars appealing their guilty verdict from a completely disadvantageous position. Because it is a disadvantage to be in prison cut off from all your resources, your attorney etc. So why do guys like Kenneth Lay and Jeffrey Skilling have all the luck? Why does the government let them go and not others? Why does society let them all get away with it? There is not one easy answer or solution that is for certain. But just because we can't come up with that all encompassing answer doesn't mean we can't do something other than what is happening right now. Certainly inordinately long prison sentences for certain people is not right, but where do you draw the line? Why was one person, me for example, given a harsher sentence than Martha Stewart? If anything I was more in need of a prison sentence like the one she got. But this isn't my personal gripe session. All in all I don't have that much to gripe about. What follows are my observations about the border, immigration and the bureau of prisons. I could have written a dry factual book that would have bored you, or it could have been some fiction piece like a John Grisham novel. This is a book about morals and how they are destroying not uplifting our country. These stories are true, to the best of my knowledge, and each one represents a different way our society's morals are impacting and impacted by individuals and the choices they make. The moral conclusion is not always presented, it is for you to arrive at.

From the outside you would never think that morals would exist in prison. On the inside prison morals can be extreme. Prisoners, for the most part, respect their elders. They make them as comfortable as could be in such a situation. They look down upon child molesters and even tend to inflict further judgment and punishment on them(most everyone has a child they love in their lives and thinks it unconscionable that such a thing should ever happen). If you lie to someone you are not going to get away with it, the confines of prison are such that they will eventually find out.

Whereas society at large as I like to call it can take a very long time to impose "justice" on the law breaker, the consequences for your actions once in prison are dealt with rapidly. Be it the prison itself through one of its agents, the guards or others, or be it by the prisoners themselves, prison justice moves swiftly.

If you had no money when you arrived in prison you were given a prison issue toothbrush, paste, soap and the lowest quality plastic razor that was more apt to cut your face than shave your whiskers. After that, each prison is different in the way it handles the procuring and dispensing of resources to inmates.

At MCC each prisoner had to have his own roll of toilet paper which was handed out on Tuesday mornings. Two rolls a week were issued to each inmate, unless they ran out. One time they did; for five days over Labor Day. If you didn't have toilet paper saved up you were shit out of luck so to speak and had to shower the shit off your ass- for five days straight. Some inmates would horde rolls of toilet paper. When the guards came around to do their periodic "random" searches they would take away all but the two you were allowed.

Out of approximately (the number fluctuated daily) 200 men on the 7th floor I'd say 175 were Mexican and/or Latino. The other 25 were white, black, Korean or Russian, literally and specifically. The racial barriers are hard and true. In prison you stick with your own kind. If you don't you can cause trouble or you can keep trouble from happening. It works both ways in prison.

I was lucky. Being both a Spanish and English speaker I was able to intermingle between the racial boundaries within the pretrial unit of this prison without having to worry too much about disrupting prison politics. This gave me some safety. No established politics could be made on the seventh floor because we were all waiting for trial. It gave me a degree of respect from the other inmates and also some of the guards.

I became a sounding board for inmates and their stories. It

made no difference to me at the time who anybody was in this place. The color of your skin which mattered so much to the rest of the inmates was of no importance to me. I just wanted to get out of here. I am glad I patiently listened to them all. Their stories represent so many others untold. Different circumstances, places but the same issues over and over. Someone like me down on their luck, maybe having just lost everything, and makes a wrong choice, a nice person forced into committing a crime through black-mail, or a greedy person just keeps on scheming new ways to get more money. All crime boils down to money or the lack there of. Plain and simple.

The Russians, all three of them, supposedly didn't speak English and they did a good job at it. They were on some Russian fishing trawler caught with 2 tons of cocaine or something like that. They were really quiet about their situation. And so will I be. No need to talk about the Russian mob, that's a topic for another book. All I will say is when I'd go to the law library they'd hand me a "kite" to give to one of their other defendants they had been separated from for trial purposes. A "kite" is a note or communiqué of any sort. Before I'd leave the unit I'd be searched for things like that but I had figured out a way to hide it so the guards never found a thing. It wasn't because I was that much smarter, its because they were by and large lazy and stupid.

Because I went to the law library frequently I became a messenger for many people and thus became "politically" important on my floor. A resource for all. And because of that I was honored and respected among the "thieves."

Blacks numbered 4 or 5. At one point a rap star came and went pretty fast, out on bail I imagine. I don't know who he was because while the racial divide wasn't that bad, it didn't exactly permit me to go over to that table and ask "hey yo, what 'sup? Who are you?"

I remember talking with this one dude named Jack who lived in our corner of the range for a while. He wanted to let me know that he was going to beat his case. Everybody said that at first. He used to walk up and down between the bunk beds gleefully telling us the latest on his trial. Supposedly he had been caught trying to bring in 20 kilos of cocaine. He had decided to go to trial. By the time he got to trial and his lawyer asked the DEA to produce the evidence, the 20 kilos, the DEA said it couldn't find them. Somehow a whole twenty kilos of cocaine had disappeared from the DEA evidence room. The judge was furious, Jack's lawyer was gleeful, the DEA was disgraced and laughed out of court as the case was dismissed. That day we never saw Jack again. A guard came and rolled his stuff up. I don't blame him for not coming back up to the unit to get whatever personal affects he may have left there. What was there for him to walk out with that he couldn't find out on the street?

The bottom line was the DEA showed its true colors of corruption with Jack's case. Unfortunately I am sure his isn't the only such case like that. How do you explain to the judge in his chambers that you let a big time drug runner get away because your own people stole the evidence? Heck, how do explain that to your superiors? Because you have to explain that to somebody, unless of course your superiors stole it. In this country that is totally possible.

The Koreans numbered two and they were both in for illegal immigration. They hated each other. One was from the North apparently and the other from the South. What I had heard was that the one from the South, an eyeglass wearing intellectual type, had taken a superior attitude to the one from the

North even though the one from the North was much bigger and threatening. So then the one from the North hated him back. Its interesting to see that their situation on an individual level represents the situation between their two countries across the sea and so far away from them.

The "Woods", the nickname given to whites, numbered anywhere from 12 to 15 and they were definitely running scared. On the outside whites outnumber any racial or ethnic group, for the time being. Here on the inside we were the minority. Most border runners who are white get sucked into doing these things out of need due to their impoverished state.

Irish was a divorcee who had just got caught for the second time trying to run cocaine across the border. He was down and out on his luck ever since his divorce. His ex was hammering him financially and had taken everything away from him and still wanted alimony. So to make it all happen he had to run drugs across the border to make ends meet because getting a "real job" with a "reputable" corporation doesn't pay anymore. At least not enough to pay off an ex and a divorce attorney and be able to still put a roof over your head in San Diego. I suppose if you were a corporate bigwig making a six figure income then maybe you could make it all work without having to do border runs or some other type of crime. But how many people are there like that and how many jobs are there like that in San Diego? Irish just needed a little validation in his life when he was going through a hard time with his divorce. Maybe if there had been some kind of resources like a male divorcee support group or something Irish would not have been doing what he had been doing. He was so in need of somebody, anybody to validate him that he would walk around the prison range interrupting your conversation to tell you how he could have done whatever it was you happened to be talking about better than you. He'd draw roses on people's envelopes for something at the prison store. Prison art. I got one for my wife's birthday. But poor Irish, his woman took it all away from him and society let him down and all he felt like he could do to rectify the situation was run drugs.

Donovan, a middle-aged alcoholic with a landscaping business, was in for tax fraud and aiding and abetting illegal immigrants whom he had hired to work for him. He got out on bail pretty quick. He had a bad skin condition that started when he arrived at MCC and no matter what he tried, even the medicine they gave him from the third world prison clinic, nothing worked. I told him it was stress related and as soon as he got out it would go away. I even showed him some yoga postures and acupressure points to help. That cheered him up. I bet half of all landscapers and construction workers in San Diego and Southern California and possibly right on up the coast to Washington are Latinos. But somehow the system picked on Donovan this year.

There was this young punk they called Carcass. He smelled like rotting flesh all the time. When you are withdrawing from methamphetamine use your body smells just as bad as when you cook it. He was so concerned with making divisions between blacks, whites and Mexicans that when I had first arrived he came up to me and asked me to choose sides. He felt threatened by my Spanish speaking and wanted to know firstly if I was a "wood" and secondly "if when the shit goes down with the Mexicans whose side you gonna run with?"

"Um, I have one side I'm runnin' with there buddy," I told him, "that's mine."

"Yeah, well we'll see how long that lasts," he said as he

started to do these military style push ups in front of me as if to impress me.

In my mind he represents every part of our society failing. Illiterate, full of hate and racist fear. How, as the world's greatest nation, did we let things get so bad for people like Carcass? Why, if we're so smart, haven't we as a collective consciousness figured out how to provide a meaningful existence and meaningful work that pays a decent wage for all our citizens? Its almost as if capitalism isn't working. Years ago the Russians gave up communism and embraced Capitalism as if to say; "Ok show us how great Capitalism is and how it works so great for you." What have we shown the Russians since they gave up communism? By the way true communism hasn't existed yet on the face of the earth, only on paper. Notwithstanding, young men who otherwise could have been valid, participating members of our great society instead find themselves looking at 8 years on the inside because they thought selling meth would solve financial problems. Who is at fault?

Swanson, what a sad story. Supposedly the law says they can't arrest you and try you anymore for something that happened more than ten years back, unless it is a capital offense. So this guy Swanson had been caught over ten years ago for trying to bring in some Mexican pot. He had been released on bail and split for Mexico again. Over ten years later he wanted to come back to the country because he was 56 years old, ill with cancer and wanted to get treatment. So instead of honoring its own laws our government violated him and until his lawyer could work things out for him he was going to have to post bail again to get out and get his treatment. Much like my story, he had nobody to post his bail even though he had a sister he had helped for years who was now rich. I used to give my fruit to Swanson sometimes because fruit helps the immune system. His sister finally came through for him and one morning he was called out and gone before I could say goodbye. Imagine being ill with cancer in prison where the medical care is as bad as that of the Third World. Stuck there because your own family refuses to be there for you?

Chuck, this border(line) schizoid, was a total asshole. For those of you who know or remember he was the fall guy for that whole strip club scandal and San Diego Councilman scandal where they took bribes to allow a porno shop near some residential neighborhood. He was in for selling illegal guns to the club owners. Mac 10's supposedly. He was always complaining about everything in prison. He was a "hard timer". He wanted everybody else to listen to him and how unfair it was and how they hadn't caught him with the guns assembled, they were still in pieces. But none of us bought it. We could tell he was a ruthless killer who hadn't been caught for murder yet. Now maybe never. If he was sentenced for 20 years he would surely die in prison.

Indio was part Apache, part Mexican and part Italian mobster (so he said, tend to doubt the Italian part.) Really nice guy, very helpful. When I first arrived there he wanted to help me and I was worried he wanted to do me sexually in return or something. But he was straight and straight up honorable. He helped me the first weeks I was there when I had no money and no way to call anybody. He lent me soups or just was there to talk to. He helped a lot of Mexicans and was heavily involved in prison politics. Somehow he had a guitar, the only one on the floor and he got me a chess set. He also ran a football lottery there every weekend. Entry was two soups per person and if you won, you ended up with thirty soups or so. I won one weekend when the Chargers lost to New England. Boy there were some pissed off people. My number was 5 which was usually a hard number to win with and everybody hated New England which is where I am from. Indio grinned real wide at me as he brought me the laundry bag full of soups. That was a good week for me. I think I almost started to gain weight that week and had it not been for my vegetarian diet I would have.

Indio was in for lots about the border, too much to really tell here. I will say he was looking at doing 20 to 30 years. I tried to check on him recently and found out he was dead. Probably killed on the inside by the mob so he wouldn't talk. I think he knew he was a marked man because he was always trying to be so nice and friendly to everybody as if he was trying to forestall having any enemies within the general prison population. He and I used to sit up nights telling stories and cracking jokes. He really helped the time go by faster for me.

When a man's family leaves him behind and society does too, a man will find his own "family" from those with whom he finds himself surrounded. The more you are surrounded by people willing to risk life, limb and liberty, the more you find yourself willing to do it and the next thing you know you are in prison.

John, a seventy year old insurance salesman, was supposedly in for fraud and they had denied him bail. If he didn't do his crime and he was right, then how horrible of the government to be so cruel and ruthless with an old man at the end of his life. If he did do it then how sad that at the end of his life he decided to do something really unnecessary.

He became my bunkie and between him, me and Indio we had a nice tight knit little corner area of "friends". I'm pretty sure he's still on the seventh floor to this day, a 70 year old man denied bail. I wonder how Kenneth Lay and Jeffrey Skilling would feel if they were denied bail while they awaited trial because they were a flight risk. Why are they still out anyway? They were convicted already. This sends a really bad message to the country; if you're rich and connected you don't go to jail even after you've been convicted because, well, you are appealing your conviction after all, and you may still be innocent yet! You may not be guilty while you are appealing the guilty verdict. What does that make of the plenty of men who have been convicted and their cases are being appealed as they sit in prison right now doing time while they await their appeals process? Shouldn't Kenny boy and Jeffrey join them? Or why shouldn't those nameless masses in prison be set free pending their appeals too?

"Curly" was supposedly fighting some murder rap involving an organized group and looked like he was going to lose. He wouldn't talk to me about it much, but he eventually got 14 years for whatever it was. What society doesn't understand is that this was a 14 year old stuck inside a 32 year old body, and that with this fourteen year old also comes a rough and tumble attitude learned from years of living on the street. So when somebody accepted him as a "brother", into a "brotherhood" type of situation, he felt honored that somebody could identify with him and be there for him during a time of need. In this situation loyalty to the group is phenomenal. His case is the perfect example of the grown man still acting like a child. In the middle of the night he used to do these body slams on the cement floor that would send the guard running they were so loud.

Although Curly and I talked a lot he never discussed his case with me. I was glad he didn't because I saw how much he fretted over it. I didn't talk with you about your case unless you asked me to look at your paperwork, which mostly only Mexicans did so they could have me translate for them. Unless you talked to me about it, I knew nothing about your situation. And mostly it was better that way. The emotional vibes of 200 stressing men was enough.

Aside from Curly and John and a mafia guy, the rest of the

whites were in MCC for trying to cross the border with drugs or illegals. They were poor and in a couple of cases had been street people. Guys otherwise down and out who were recruited by the Mexican gangs to do runs across the border. That was the only reason a white guy got caught running the border at all; because he was down and out on his luck, like me. A couple of these white guys were messed up in the head from life circumstances that must have just kept hammering them further and further down until somebody came to them and asked them if they wanted to run the border.

If our country would truly provide equal opportunities for all and elevate the poorest of our society then no one would be doing border runs. I am sure of it. I remember working for a company once that had the motto "our team is only as strong as the weakest member." Maybe our country, society and government should think about that instead of pointing fingers, placing blame and looking for scapegoats, wasting money all the way. Make our weakest link a valid member of society with a job that pays a decent wage to live life, not just survive life.

Many Mexicans are also coerced into participating in running the border. Either literally forced to carry a kilo or two of drugs for their coyote as part of their deal to being led to a better life or preyed upon in some other way due to their specific circumstances.

Most of the honest Mexicans who get caught trying to cross the border in pursuit of a "legitimate" American dream never have their stories told. Their stories are wrapped up into one mega-story told by the media and only from the perspective of where they are from how they got here and how they are getting back. Nothing is said about what happens to them when they are in the prison system or how and under what situations they are returned to their country of origin. Nothing is said about people crossing the border many times and having nothing happen to them even though they have been caught nine or ten times before the government finally punishes them.

Meanwhile, others, for some unexplainable reason are given the shaft so "we can make an example of them." But lets be quite honest, the general public is not interested in knowing about all the gory details of this great dirty shame we call the border and what happens there.   Most people don't realize that it started long ago in the 1920's and has been going on ever since. They don't want to be reminded of the decades of fruits and vegetables harvested, picked by the economic slaves we call illegal aliens. For to be reminded of this would leave a bad taste in their mouths as they swallowed this illegal food. For this food could be considered illegal. If you know it was picked by illegal aliens and you buy it you are an accessory to a crime after the fact. Its time to stop eating or start thinking for yourselves and not let a government confuse you about what's right and wrong.

This whole scenario at the border is an ugly reminder of the fascism which has gripped this country for some time now and how it doesn't want to let go of its hold on power. Caught in the crossfire of this national discrimination, are the Mexicans, other illegals and poor whites from this side. Those mostly caught in the crossfire and at risk of being sent home to a bleaker existence are the Mexicans. You never hear about the illegal Swedish immigrants here after their student visas expired and how they didn't want to go home because life is so much worse for them there in Sweden. They simply overstay their visa and leave when they want and nobody cares. Substitute any other person like that who is basically white and in the same situation. White and privileged that's what can keep you out, sometimes. But once in prison white and scared.

If there was such a thing as your favorite time of day in prison, mine would have to be early morning. It was quiet and the TV wasn't on yet. Nobody was talking or singing or arguing. No games being played. No nothing. Just a lot of snoring. Some mornings more than others. All the guards were respectful of that quiet, all but one.

I had the top bunk and for the duration of my stay I was continually climbing up or jumping down. Once up I tried to stay up for a while just because it was a hassle to jump up and down all the time. In the beginning I did a lot of sleeping, or tried to. The bed I had was right next to the TV. As soon as the TV was on in the morning I was awake and the volume was always on the highest setting.

The eight ranges on the floor were arranged around a common area. They each had a bathroom and three showers. Each range had a metal barred door. When it was "lock down" time you just went to your range with the other 50 or so men and they locked you in for the night or the afternoon. So it wasn't so bad, not like being locked up in a tiny cell with nowhere to walk. In the morning, at 5:30 they opened up the range doors to let us out for breakfast and to get hot water for coffee and walk around. Breakfast was a dismal affair which consisted of a half pint of milk and a little box of some kind of corn flakes or Special K if you were lucky. Some mornings a scoop of hot oatmeal or farina was there. With that came a little bit of some poorly made cake and a sour apple, rotting banana or tasteless orange. If you didn't get up for breakfast you didn't get it. Most mornings I didn't bother with it even though I was up. If I did it was only to get fruit to give away. Mostly I didn't like waiting in lines, especially early in the morning when all I was waiting for was a crappy breakfast. The meal times interfered with my yoga practice anyway- nothing worse than doing yoga on a stomach full of crap. Lunch and dinner were at 10a.m. and 4p.m. respectively- bad times for yoga practices. If I could get lunch and dinner and save it I would so that later when my yoga practice was over I could eat. But a lot of the time a guard prevented me from taking food back to my range unless I hid it in my jump-suit. There was no good rationale for not allowing you to take your food back to your bunk since we all had food in our lockers from the prison store. It was just to mess with us.

There were lots of tables in the common area with attached seats to them. So in the early morning you could have a peaceful moment writing letters or drinking coffee etc. Some would get their morning walk in by walking the outer perimeter of the common area. Doing laps helped keep the body healthy.

After initially being told I couldn't, I had finally been given the o.k. to do my yoga practice. The guards didn't like that I could stand on my head. In the beginning they had told me I couldn't do yoga in the unit. That was until the prison chaplain told them they had to let me- and anywhere I wanted to too. It was a violation of my freedom of religion if they didn't. I didn't tell them yoga wasn't a religion but a science, but they, including the chaplain were unaware. And I was given a letter from the chaplain to show to any guard who didn't know yet. But I was told I could not teach yoga to anybody. So if I did I had to do so on the sly. I'm not sure why sharing an exercise practice that not only made the body feel better but energized the spirit was such a taboo thing in a place filled with bummed out men.

Today I was finally getting out on bail. My bail had been set ridiculously low as if to tease me, because nobody would help with their signature. A signature bail. Nobody had to pay anything, just a signature. Nobody would step up to the plate. Not my family, not my wife's. (I found out later that my father-in-law not only wouldn't help but lied to my wife and told her I had no bail).

This morning like every other morning here I started off with my meditation until I heard the door open. Once the door opened, the others got in line for breakfast and started to get their coffees ready for hot water and stake out their part of the tables for their friends after breakfast was over. Even here, people acted all political about things. Vying for what little resources were available to them. Hording tasteless coffee cake or fruit. Buying pieces of chicken for postage stamps for example. People claiming rights to plastic chairs, televisions, decks of cards or chess sets. I learned my lesson fast about that one. I like to play chess and when I first got there I asked this one sureno if I could borrow his set. He said sure as long as I returned it to him. So I played and then when it was time, returned it to him. About fifteen minutes later he came to me with a different set, one that was all tore up, and accused me of trying to give him back the wrong set to keep the good one for myself. Of course I hadn't. He was just looking to cause trouble. He told me if I didn't give him back his set he was going to kick my ass. I told him I gave him the correct set and he was trying to pull a fast one on me. Then he acted like I had called him a liar, which he was, and threatened me even more. So I ignored him.

Later this guy named Diablo, also a sureno, came to talk to me. He told me he had straightened it out and to get my own chess set in the future to avoid these kinds of situations. Later on I did get my own set from Indio. So much trouble I had in prison over chess sets. Diablo was funny though. He had a tattoo across the back of his neck that said "DIABLO" and "sureno" written across his stomach. He was 22 years old and was looking at 15 years or something crazy like that for trying to bring in illegals for the umpteenth time. As he told me, "its ok homey, me and my buddies will take control of these federal tax dollars and put them to good use and we'll run this show up in here all across the country. And we'll do whiteys up the poop chute all day long until we get released." He had already been in for two years with the State and it was almost like a status symbol for him to be here "in the Feds."

Diablo is right about the Latinos controlling the prison system. In any given location within the prison system there are more Latinos than anybody else. They do have control over the resources spent there. If they wanted to watch television and a white guy was there first, the Mexicans would just change the channel on him and he'd either have to watch what they wanted or walk away. The MCC Administration had to post signs saying equal access to the TVs, but they weren't respected and Mexicans dominated the airwaves in the unit.

I remember when I first got to the seventh floor how scared I was. The whole floor was locked down and I was the only new guy to walk into the main common area. I had to sit and wait at one of the tables. All the inmates were pressed up against the bars to see who I was. They were all shouting.

"Vaselina para el Nuevo!" "Vaseline for the new guy!" I seriously thought I was going to get it up the ass so I didn't sleep that night.

Later I changed it to "Vaselina para tus huevos!" "Vaseline for your balls!" Because almost everybody who had been at MCC for any length of time had jock itch.

But seriously, how scary it was for somebody who had never been in the prison system before. I had led a good life for the most part and was certainly not gay. What a shocking welcome it was and my goodbye was just as loud and riotous. Anytime anybody yelled that or the other expression we came to know oh so well, I would just give my Mexican war cry "Aaaaah Haaaaaa

Aiiiiiiiii!" That was louder than anything anybody else could belt out seeing as my yogic lungs could carry more volume with so much air in them.

I hopped down off my top bunk that morning as I usually did, like a cat, always carefully landing square on my feet. My knee bothered me today but I jumped down anyway. One thing in prison; don't show any weakness, physical or mental, because, if you do, eventually someone will use it against you and eat you up.

At my locker I prepared my donated plastic container (previously inhabited by Keefe peanut butter) with Keefe instant Columbian coffee and two C&H sugar packets.

By now everybody knew my morning routine; yoga for 45 minutes, then the shop was open. I had been here on the seventh floor for 8 weeks and by now anybody knew to come to me if they needed help with a letter or translation. In return I would get a pack of ramen soup or something. If they were really poor and I knew it I would help them for free. If nobody needed help I'd play chess.

I'd do my yoga practice right there next to my bunk before anything else, then it was upstairs to the common area to find whatever part of the tables hadn't been contested there. After I sat down to play chess and help others with their thoughts and cases etc. my day would go by fast.

Officer Larios had been giving me the paper and so I read articles of interest out loud in Spanish to the others. Articles about the border or about Mexico. Aside from that mostly I played chess.

One of the Mexicans I played chess with was this illegal who had been caught several times before for jumping the border. This time he had been caught robbing a bank on this side in addition to his illegal status in the U.S. Nobody had beaten me for quite some time, but this guy did through some distractive trickery and then boasted to everybody how he beat Richard Simmons. By the way, being the spitting image of Richard Simmons when he was younger was something you'd think wouldn't be to your advantage in prison, but somehow I managed to make it work. But when I challenged this bank robber to a rematch and whooped up on him good, he went to the bathroom and took one of those plastic razor's blade out of the plastic and tried to slit his wrists. At first I thought it was the humiliation of having been beaten by one of the only white guys on the floor and one who looked like Richard Simmons! Someone told me during the resultant lockdown, because we got locked down during his removal to the psych ward, that he had just come from the psych ward and was on psych meds and that he was looking at doing a minimum of 12 years for armed robbery and illegal entry. When your life is collapsing in on you from all sides any little thing can break you.

Weeks before I had beaten a Paisa named Jalisco. He was the leader of the Paisa gang on the 7th floor. He had challenged me too, but for postage stamps because that's how its done inside. I didn't have a lot of money so I didn't risk it. I beat him of course but later that day the North Korean guy played him a game of pool and lost. When he didn't have the money Jalisco sodomized him that night while six or seven Mexicans held him down in the bathroom. That was a somber moment for him because he was a big North Korean. He came to me later and asked me to translate for him. I told him no because it didn't matter. He should just roll up his stuff and wait by the door for the guard to come. They call it "rolling it up" in prison. He eventually did roll up and stand by the door as the whole cell block roared "hilo."

When I first heard this word "hilo" I could not understand for the life of me what the hell they were saying. "Hilo" is an expression that only has local significance. In Spanish hilo is the word for thread or string. But to the uneducated population of Tijuana it means "get lost" or "string it on out of here." So anytime anybody did something wrong or stupid, the whole cell block would yell "HILO." The only other time I heard it used was when somebody was being released on bail or leaving the unit a "free" man.

I asked somebody later why Jalisco would want to do that kind of thing to a big Korean dude. They told me because he was looking at doing a very long time in prison and the Korean's butt was smooth and hairless. See, in Mexico a man who gets another man to perform a sexual act for them is not gay. They call him a "mayate" or something like that. Curiously enough "mayate" is also the word used for blacks. I don't know why and I couldn't find a single Mexican to explain it to me. Only the man who is doing the sexual act upon the other is considered gay. It's all very strange and when you try to talk to somebody about it they get all flustered. Its an interesting cultural twist on ancient Greek and Roman cultures.

Whites were looked down upon in MCC. Most white guys were burnt out border runners. Some were high class insurance scammers or check fraud or wire fraudsters. But the border runners were usually homeless dudes from San Diego or Southern California who were down and out hard on their luck. Its that way all across the border and on both sides. The border is a vortex for evil.

There was this Mexican dude they called Tijuas. What a nightmare for this guy. He had been caught crossing the border with a small quantity of pot, 80 pounds. No really that's small. You only get three months in prison for that as a first time offense. So anyway, while he's in prison in Arizona somebody commits a crime in California with the same name and social security number he used. So since he is in custody somehow they transfer him to MCC and he has to stand trial for a crime he could not have possibly committed seeing as he was in prison at the time the crime was committed. The government doesn't care. Once you are in prison they convict you of crimes even easier. Since you are already an inmate they do not even have to let you appear in court if they do not want to. This makes it so you need more time in the law library and have to petition the court via mail from prison. You rarely get to see the judge unless you file a writ of habeas corpus. But even then they don't have to let you appear at the "reading of the writ." Heck its not even read except in the privacy of a judge's chambers. No public reading in court. Good luck trying to get a press release when you're the average joe in prison looking for a little justice on the inside. Trust me, nobody cares. So poor Tijuas may very well get convicted of a crime he didn't commit and the system is too blind to care. I've been helping him file his paperwork since I got here and it looks like there may be a little light at the end of the tunnel; If he pleads to a lesser charge for the crime he could not have committed then the prosecutor agreed to recommend giving him only six additional months in prison!

"Pops" was a senior citizen who had been left behind by this country. With no relatives, and not enough social security income to get him by month to month, he started running marijuana across the border. He had been doing it for years since his "retirement". He had been caught once before and this time he was looking at doing six years. He was my dad's age, 79. He had a girlfriend in Tijuana, a mobile home and a bunch of stuff he'd saved up since he "retired". Again, if this country, supposedly the best in the world, would just provide a decent living situation to its seniors, maybe they wouldn't be in such dire straights as to need to do something like that. As a senior I can see why you would not be thrilled at the prospect of working at Burger King at the age of 79. I mean come on now. How could you do that to an old man?

I remember the day Pops found out how much time he was looking at doing in prison. He was on his bunk, a lower bunk across from mine, being consoled by John. He and John bunked below me and made up our little corner of the 8th Range. Indio was the fourth one of us in that corner. Above Pops' bunk was one Mexican dude or another, they kept coming and going as time went on; catch and release. Chuck was in the top bunk above Indio. Between me and Indio we looked after these two old guys Pops and John. But poor Pops, when he found out it was probably going to do six years he broke down blubbering his head off. Right before he had found out, he had called a friend in Tijuana and found out his girl had split and his RV was gone. At that moment I am sure he knew he would die in prison without a penny to his name. The survival rate for elderly inmates is really low and if he did get out there was nothing for him to return to or to do or have at the age of 85. Imagine 85 and living on the streets of San Diego. There are no official numbers on the survival rate of elderly inmates because the BOP doesn't want to know much less tell you.

This other old dude couldn't make it out of bed one day. In fact he couldn't make it to the bathroom to take a leak. So he barely made it up and over to a trashcan and peed in it. The guards got so upset they threw him in the hole for peeing into the trashcan. What they didn't realize was that they should have taken him to medical. He died in the hole. But hey, it was an old street bum with nobody on the outside to even claim his body. No lawsuit, no liability. Who cares, right?

Aside from these two elderly dudes, Indio, me and the others whom I already mentioned, the other whites were street junkies. One guy, Ed, called "Special Ed", was a street person from San Diego who was caught right at the checkpoint trying to give a ride to some Mexicans. He had been stopped many times before. But each time he had declared right away and nothing had happened. Finally Customs and Immigration got so angry with him that they decided to finally charge him. By the time he was processed and sentenced it would be time served and he was gone.

He was bald and had this big mustache across his face. I thought he looked like a squid with that bald head and big eyes, slightly parted as if he was the victim of fetal alcohol syndrome. He had had a lung taken out a year earlier and the general thought around the unit was he wasn't getting enough oxygen to the brain. He wasn't. He was always short of breath and always had this strange smell to him, like he was one stage before death or something. To make matters worse, poor Special Ed thought he needed some extra money and had started selling his butt to the Mexicans. At first it had started out as a really bad joke the Mexicans played on him. He had lost a bet and so the Mexicans formed a ring and he ran around butt naked while they slapped his butt as he ran by them in the circle. After that somebody tossed him a bag of pork rinds. Add slight insanity to Special Ed's missing lung problem and you have a mind twisted enough to turn that into a money making scheme which concluded with a Mexican in his butt for 25 top ramen noodle soups. By the way, a pack of ramen noodle soup at the prison commissary in

MCC is 25 cents. So for $12.50 in prison Special Ed prostituted himself. The funny thing was he had a month till he was to be released, time served.

Some of the other whites came to me and asked me to talk with the Mexicans because they were afraid the Mexicans would get the wrong idea and want to go around looking for some other white ass. Funny thing was, between myself and this other big white biker dude we were what would be called the shot callers for the whites. Each group has a "shot caller" the one who calls the shots. So me, shot caller by default, because on our floor I participated in none of that gang stuff. If someone tried to drag me into that vibe I said no. They tried, whites and Mexicans both.

I went to one of the "shot callers" for the Mexicans who was a "friend" of mine and like me was shot caller by default. I explained the situation. I told him how Ed was this guy about to get released and that he was messed up in the head and just needed to be left alone because, after all, who knew if he had AIDS.

Octavo agreed with me but recommended I go to Ed and tell him not to provoke anything before he leaves.

When I went to Ed, the poor guy was sitting on his bunk. He had a bottom bunk due to his missing lung. I sat down on the bunk across from his. It belonged to a Mexican who had given me the nod.

I told Ed straight up. I didn't want to even hear the vaguest rumor that he was doing that ever again or I'd get him rolled up and send a message to whichever floor he ended up on that they should play him out hard until he gets out. To Special Ed this was real. He was so messed up mentally that he actually thought I was a shot caller especially because he knew I was fully bilingual and appeared to have a lot of juice around the joint.

Of course I was doing it for him. He had a month left. And I told him so. "Ed, why the hell would you do something like that with a month left? And if you are going to do something like that at least wait until you get out and make more money at it on the street and don't jeopardize us."

He agreed. That was yesterday. Today I get out but he doesn't know that. Special Ed's story is a glaring example of how society is failing us. Here is a man who just lost a lung. He needs some help. Obviously something else is going on with him and he could use a hand figuring out some right conduct for himself. Instead he'll be thrown in some homeless shelter they have down there in San Diego that the community is very proud of. I have worked in homeless shelters and I can tell you that most are one step above being a prison. Since I've been in prison too I can tell you that in all qualified honesty. Homeless shelters are generally not places from where people rise up again. They are way stations to failure. Poor Special Ed should have had somebody there for him so he didn't make his mistakes.

The federal government wouldn't care if he violated the terms of his probation, he's a street person from San Diego. This is where "recidivism rates" come into play. Ed will violate probation just by simply not finding and establishing a residence. Then, if the Federal government feels like imposing sanctions on him for having violated probation they just find him and pick him up. But maybe they don't find him. He's a street person after all. So they'll never see him again until he gets in trouble the next time. Once Ed does violate, he will become part of the 65% of all federal inmates who do go back to prison on a violation. That's what's called the recidivism rate. All it means is heaps more trouble for poor folks and heaps more tax dollars from rich folks. All to mess with guys like Special Ed, instead of spending the resources on helping him out in the first place.

The people on the right will tell you that high recidivism rates mean that parole and probation programs must be working. That they are designed to catch people violating the term of their parole or probation. They will leave it at that and hope they don't have to get into any specifics with you about recidivism. The people on the left will tell you that high recidivism rates mean that parole and probation isn't working because the terms and conditions of parole and probation are designed to set the inmate up for failure. Before I had my experience I wouldn't have been able to say either way. But since I am a qualified opinion holder on this matter I can honestly say that I feel very lucky. I beat the odds.

As part of the terms and conditions of my release I had to hold a 40 hour a week job (very difficult to work around my wife's schedule and childcare issues). I was not allowed to go to school either, only work. If I didn't hold a regular full time job I would go back to prison. As an ex-con the types of jobs available to me and the pay rate they offered were dismal. Not very motivating for me to work. If I moved or lost my job I had to report this to my probation officer within three days and if I didn't it would be a violation of my probation and I would go back to prison. Luckily I had my wife and two boys waiting for me when I finally got out. Most men don't have that. They've been in so long their wives and families have moved on and they have been forgotten. Just those two simple requirements holding a job and getting and keeping a place to stay can be the most difficult for an ex-con, especially if he has no friends or family. Everywhere you look on job apps and rental apps it asks you if you've ever been convicted of a felony. After you put that on an application for housing or employment good luck!

It would be logical to assume that our Christian oriented society would find forgiveness in its heart and make it easier to find employment and housing for a member of society who had made a mistake. A member who needed a hand up to succeed in life instead of being left helpless only to violate their parole or probation.

Holding a job and keeping a place to stay may seem like something easy or basic. Tell that to the 13 million homeless in our country today. Tell that to the inmate being released tomorrow. There are other conditions of probation that make things really difficult. Your bank accounts are watched and you are required to disclose any financial transaction over $500. You must disclose your vehicular information, reporting about all vehicles owned by members of your house, their tag numbers and identification numbers, and mileage. Every month. If your crime was a drug crime you must be drug tested once a week, twice a month, its up to the judge. Should you miss any appointments, drug tests or otherwise, it would be a violation and at the sole discretion of your probation officer you go back to prison if they choose.

I can tell you that high recidivism rates are not because parole and probation are working properly. High recidivism rates exist because the parole and probation programs do not work. Combined with a lack of effective prison programs to prepare inmates for the shock of being thrust back into a society they don't know anymore, parole and probation does nothing more than help keep prison populations unnecessarily high. Please don't trust anything the prison system may say to make itself look good in the public's eye. They are desperate to keep the terrible truth a secret: its using your money to wrongfully hurt people every day.

Here's the funny part; the American Correctional Association president, Gwendolyn Chunn supposedly made this statement about a lack of trust in the prison system: "We completely reject this suggestion and will fight to ensure that corrections remains and works by the same rules that every other government agency does." Whoa! What does that mean? Since we are quite sure that all government agencies are corrupt and all high up officials are bribed regularly, then we can assume what Ms. Chunn is referring to here is that her organization is going to fight to make sure the bribery system in place for all government organizations stays the same for the B.O.P.? That sounds about right to me. But if she's talking about moral and ethical "rules", I don't trust what she says.

Octavo's, the Mexican's shot caller's, story is a movie unto itself. He was raised in Tijuana. He traveled to Japan on a computer company contract. Apparently the Japanese have a major stake in a factory just south of the border. Anyway, Octavo goes to Japan, marries a Japanese girl and brings her home. They have a baby together in San Diego so it's a US Citizen. He's working at the factory making $2000 a month in Tijuana. This is super big money. One of the drug cartels takes his little girl and tells him he has to start running drugs to the U.S. if he ever wants to see her again. So he does. Several times in one week, then gets caught. He speaks pretty good English and Japanese.

He became my friend because he didn't know much about the law and they wouldn't let him go to the law library. In fact most inmates on the 7th floor don't ever see it even though they are all pre-trial. I got on the law library list simply by privilege-for being a white English speaking citizen of this country. But Octavo, he fought tooth and nail and won. He told the courts he had bought a car recently and taken it to a shop in Tijuana. They didn't have the part he needed, they told him it was in San

Diego. He was on his way to go to the other shop in San Diego when they busted him and "he had no idea it had marijuana in it." The guys from the shop in Tijuana must have loaded it up for their buddies at the other shop etc. etc. Final word- not guilty.(found that out after I got out). During the time leading up to my getting out he had me help him prepare a petition for a pardon so he could be a citizen after all. That was in the event he lost.

Its amazing to think just how many smart people are in prison. I know we always say 'well, must not have been smart enough....otherwise he wouldn't be in prison," but the fact that they got caught just means the government spent a ton of resources just to apprehend the few that they do catch. Because I'll tell you, one half of all federal inmates are Latino, mostly Mexican. It's a real trip. And because of the situation with the border between cities like Tijuana and San Diego, as I said, the prison population at a border prison like MCC is 90% Latino. At least on the 7th floor, the pretrial unit.

Lots of inmates still sleeping at this hour. Its nice, almost. Time for some quiet reflection before the fiesta starts for the day. The rounds of ramen soups and instant refried beans. Chips salsa. Little pepperoni sticks and liquid cheese. Soda pop and ice from the ice machine if you wanted (it was always a little risky when you had two hundred men delving into it all day every day).   Of course the real meals they served you three times a day didn't cut it, and on purpose. Here at MCC the government doesn't want to spend too much because the resources are almost all being used for illegals. The price the government pays a federal contractor per meal is something like $2.50 per meal. The cost to the contractor is like .25 cents. For lunch if you are lucky you get a mealy apple, some wilted iceberg lettuce and a small shriveled up hot dog, hamburger or some other unrecognizable meat product. For dinner it was pretty much the same. The government wants it that way so people have to have money sent to them there so they can eat well. That way they spend money at the prison store to supplement their diet. If you have no money you start losing weight fast. Like me. When I came in 8 weeks ago I was around 190 pounds. When I got out on bail I was 165 pounds.

The prison store is really big business. Microwave popcorn is a big money maker at 75 cents a bag. On some of the items the mark up may be modest but on things like popcorn its huge. Popcorn being a small ticket item, almost everybody who has money buys a bag of popcorn when they go to the store. And there are something like 350,000 inmates in the BOP (that's not including state and county facilities.) So if just half of them buy two bags of microwave popcorn a week (you're allowed up to six in most prisons) times 60 cents in profit for each bag, that's $210,000 a week on popcorn alone. That's the low estimate. Same with ramen noodle soups. In the store on the outside the retail price is 10 cents. In prison its 25 to fifty cents depending on which prison you are at. And everybody who has money buys them.

Now think about shampoo, toothpaste, shower shoes, other types of accessories even certain clothes, workout pants running shoes etc. Running shoes that cost too, $60 70 bucks. It is a total money maker. Even Ben and Jerry's and Hagen Dazz ice cream are there. Otis Spunkmeyer too. The prison system doesn't pay retail price either, it gets a bulk deal on it all. So the profit is more than we can know.

The real sinister part to the BOP prison store money making scam is so terrible that no mainstream media will even touch it. First, as if it wasn't already bad enough that the Bush family controls things like oil and drug companies, they also have to have control over contracting with the BOP. When can we get rid of these Bush people? The Keefe company, which sells just about everything from coffee to peanut butter, is supposedly part owned by the Bush family. The money spent on popcorn is nothing compared to the amount spent on Keefe products each week. The sick part is that Federal judges who have stock in companies like Keefe that contract with the BOP have a vested interest in seeing people get longer prison sentences. In all actuality no Federal judge who has stock in any company that does business with the BOP should be handing out prison terms, they should recuse themselves from the bench due to this horrendous conflict of interest. Try bringing that up at the time of your trial and you will get skewered with the harshest sentence a judge can give you just to shut you up.

Bob Barker? Well he has his own soap company that the BOP buys. Those little bars of soap you see in a hotel room. Except these little bars, given out for free to inmates who have no money, have Bob Barker's name all over the packaging. Boy am I sure glad that Adam Sandler guy punched the heck out of him in that movie. I bet Bob Barker is somewhere thinking he is doing a good thing by helping keep inmates clean, while secretly he gloats at the money he makes off the Federal prison system for some tallow soap. Who knows, the way this country is heading, next thing you know they could be using dead Mexicans for tallow in soap just like they used dead Jews for soap during the holocaust.

Telephone contact is just as big a money maker for the BOP as the prison store is, if not more so. The funny thing is all this money the BOP makes off of the inmates is supposed to go into what is called the "Prisoners' Trust account". In turn the

Prisoners' Trust account is supposed to be used for programs for the prisoners. Projects requiring educational resources inside the prison to help prepare inmates for the shock of being released into society once again. Money from the Prison Trust account is used for financial assistance to prisoners who do get released but have no money to get home, or food on the road while they are traveling back home. There are so many prisoner programs that are supposed to have been set up for the embetterment of the inmates. Music rooms, woodworking programs. Art and sports programs. But in the last couple of years the BOP Administration has said there isn't enough money to fund these prison programs. At MCC those programs are almost totally non-existent. Nothing is being offered to illegal immigrants. What few programs they do have like a meditation class and philosophy class, are all conducted in English so the illegals cannot participate. There are certainly no rehabilitative services here at MCC. We are not here to be rehabilitated one guard told me, just for storage.

Curiously enough though there is plenty of prisoner money used to fund religious services for inmates, and those are almost all exclusively Christian. Books? Tons for Christian books. But there are used beat up copies of the Koran as if to say, "see, we aren't such racist bigots after all." Here and there the occasional book on Yoga or Buddhism makes its way into the prison, and those are snatched up right away by inmates and not seen again unless you know who to ask. If the B.O.P. simply spent some of the money on the things it was supposed to there would be enough books of all faiths. There would be enough rehabilitative services to help inmates.

Oh and anybody who tells you there are adequate services, they saw them on a prison tour. What nonsense. All the tours inside prisons are so carefully scripted. Before any of these bureaucrats ever get to tour a floor the prison officials come through and force a serious cleaning out of the inmates. In one instance we were goaded into cleaning as part of a contest to see which floor in the prison could be the cleanest and we won. Our prize? A little bag of popcorn, freshly made right there in the unit! I told somebody at the time "it's the carnival!"

So the BOP saying that it has no money in the Prisoners' Trust Account is a big fat lie. Its not spending the money on the areas its supposed to-at all. Where the money goes nobody knows because there is no independent agency that has any oversight over the B.O.P. No judge, Congress nobody. The only one who can tell this shadow organization they call the B.O.P. what to do is the Attorney General himself. Maybe he should tell us where all the money is going and what is going on with the B.O.P.!

AT&T as the sole federal contractor to provide telephone services to inmates to call their loved ones. Big brother right there listening in on you too. Quite possibly if it didn't have the B.O.P. contract and other federal contracts it would be out of business. But since it does of course it is going to work in cahoots with the Feds. It enjoys all the privileges of a federal contractor.

Since AT&T knows that the inmates have no collective bargaining rights it rips the inmates off. Average in state and out of state long distance calls from your own home normally cost anywhere from 3 to 10 cents a minute these days. But the BOP and AT&T charge inmates 25 cents a minute on average to place calls to their loved ones. If it is a collect call, rates vary from $1.75 to $2.75 per minute. The words rape and pillage come to mind. Rape because AT&T is price gouging, the BOP lets them and there is nobody to stop them from doing it. Pillage because the money made off of these phone calls is supposed to go into the Prisoners' Trust Account and doesn't. But if the BOP says there isn't enough funding that means the money must be going somewhere else. Why do I say this? Well do the numbers with me; if you have 350,000 inmates making phone calls daily, weekly etc. and they are allowed to have an average of 300 phone minutes per month and AT&T is overcharging by lets say 15 cents (a low ball estimate) well then that's roughly 15.75 million dollars a month in profit. A month. That's on the low end too. So where in God's name is all that money going? We can only imagine. The BOP isn't telling. Its not going into the programs and its not possible that sports and art supplies and whatnot cost much more than that. Just one month's worth of phone calls could supply all those programs throughout the whole of the Bureau of Prisons.

Just when I'm thinking these thoughts someone comes up to talk. Its this guy they call Chanchamon, or Don Chewey. For some reason everybody thought he looked like some alien from that space wars series. He was always praying with us at night just as lights went out and before the evening count.

Out of fifty men in Ranges 7 and 8, about 23 joined hands and prayed together at night just before the ten o'clock count. We all prayed for a miracle to release us. John, my bunkie, had been leading a prayer session at night since before I arrived. Ever since I arrived I translated it in Spanish and vice versa for any Mexican who had a prayer they wanted to add. You could feel a certain energy passing through the group. The difference in our two ranges on the floor was remarkable. We prayed together and forged a sort of community. Other ranges didn't and you could tell the difference. Don Chewey was always there. John is there to this day leading the prayer.

"Hey Ritchie, como estas? How you doin?"

"Good Chewey. Que paso?"

"Ritchie me estan diciendo por alli que tu lograste sacar el Butridge de aca. Es cierto? Did you get rid of Butridge for us man? Is it true?"

"Oh, Don Chewey," I said with a grin and left it at that for a second to see what he would do if I didn't tell him. He really was a good man. They say he is a human trafficker. He didn't force twenty people into the back of his air conditioned truck. He wasn't selling them into slavery. He was just trying to help them get across the border. A human trafficker meant something else to me. Somebody who forced others into doing it. Chewy had a family to feed. It wasn't his fault that his government or the rich from his society hadn't figured out how to provide decent wages in his country. Poor guy. I think in the end they consolidated his charges into just one or two and he was looking at signing a deal for like forty months.

I told him the deal. This Officer named Rutlidge would wake everybody up at 5:00 a.m. yelling at the top of his lungs that it was time to get up even though we didn't have to be up. He was an ex Navy boy used to getting up really early and it was his way of punishing us for a crime we hadn't been convicted of yet. We were all sick and tired of him.

When they locked us down you had to run to your gate and get into your Range before they shut it. Officer Rutlidge loved to call me Richard Simmons. So a couple of days back I just barely got through the gates during a morning lockdown and count and Rutlidge said really loud;

"Come on Richard Simmons, lets go."

So I took the opportunity to call my wife not too long

after the count and told her (and the Feds listening to my phone call) that officer Rutlidge had patted me on the ass and called me Richard Simmons. Wow what an impact! Forget going to a prison official directly with a problem. You won't get anything done. Just call somebody up on the phone and tell it to that person and whamo. T

The very next day they locked down the whole damn floor and had the Lieutenant come up and question me about a possibly abusive situation. I told him how Officer Butridge (I didn't call him that to the Lieutenant, but we called him that amongst ourselves) had touched me on the ass and called me Richard Simmons as he locked us down. That was the end of Butridge. They put him on elevator duty. That's when they started calling me "Ritchie of Oz" up in this joint. No more being woken up at some god awful hour of the morning by some ex-navy officer all thanks to little ole Richard Simmons. "And a one and a two."

There was a Richard Simmons book in the prison library. Some book from the 70's when he was young and had a really big fro. Photos of him doing the "tootsie roll". Man every time I went to the library there was some inmate there pointing at the book then pointing at me. But whatever. Most inmates didn't know or didn't care. Most guards could give a shit either.

The guards were unfortunately more ignorant than some of the inmates. Mostly ex-military who couldn't get a job in the private sector for the life of them after their years of service to this unforgivable and unforgiving country. Only to start out making $2000 a month, before taxes. In San Diego that didn't get you far. So as a result you get some of the most ignorant jerks to work here. Any hope at a little compassion for the inmates was thrown out the window. The inmates used to joke with some of the guards who seemed to be a little more aware. This one guard named Ramirez got upset one time though. This young hip Mexican they called Chilango, because he was from Mexico City, told Ramirez he should quit his job and he'd get him a better one at the border as a border agent on the take. Chilango said; " make better money than the 2 grand you get for prostituting yourself out to the man."

"Couldn't be making better money than your momma in Tijuana on the streets now could I though Chilango?" said the guard. At this Chilango bristled up and said;

"Yeah, better money, but not better money than your momma makes on the streets in Compton. I heard Snoop dog did her good."

At that the guard slammed Chilango hard against the wall and had him cuffed up and on the floor in no time waiting for an escort to the hole. They locked us down for that one of course. People go to the hole because most of the time they deserve to. Other times its just guards superimposing their will on an inmate they don't like.

The hole. Otherwise known as SEG (Segregated, which is a term they don't like to use anymore) or SHU(Solitary Housing Unit) or Solitary. The real horrible truths about the hole could never completely come out because it would expose the true ugliness of the human condition. To do so one would have to get all inmates former and current who have been to the hole to give their testimony. But the BOP and the secret minions of the Federal government, the Trilateralists, Illuminati, Freemasons, Builderbergers and the infamous Skull and Bones society would hunt those inmates down. They would kill them before they ever gave their testimony. And if they couldn't do that, they would at the very least find something illegal that they've done again and have them tossed back in prison before they could ever give testimony for the cruel atrocities committed in our nation's prisons every day. To be sure inmates themselves often precipitate guard backlashes. And the few stories that follow are primarily of inmates being totally nutty, even before they get to the hole.

A guy just gets back from the hole where they had him for a couple of weeks. He was in a cell about six feet by 15 or 17 feet with a bunk bed and two plastic mattresses on the floor as well. A "hole" for four. See, most times when you go to the hole you are put in with others. This is part of the punishment. Four men in a small confined area with an open toilet in the corner is going to eventually get to you in some way. Only those in protective custody get their own cell. Everybody else gets - the shaft.

So the guy who gets back from the hole tells us some really nutty stories about what is going on down there. There are these two brothers who were in for some crazy double murder of some FBI agents or something. They were looking at doing life anyway so they were not too concerned with being good. They were called Big and Little Wick. One day Big Wick's old lady came to visit him. Now, everywhere throughout the BOP the visiting rooms and rules differ. The visiting rooms at MCC have video cameras everywhere. There is no guard in the room unless something is happening and they don't need one because they can just monitor the situation through their multiple video cameras. So Big Wick's in there with his old lady. Well, we are talking about a three hundred pound man and an equally big Mama. And what do they do? They start going to town. Big Wick doin' his ole lady doggie style over a table. You can imagine the look on that guard's face watching his monitor show these monstrous people pressing the flesh together. And you can imagine what it must have been like for these guards to have to go in there and pull them apart and take them away.

But what happened next was even worse. If you hit a prison guard its an extra five years in prison and all that happens is you appear before the judge and they give you the five years because nobody is going to believe you otherwise. But if you are already looking at life then who the hell cares right? So Big Wick got put in his own cell because he told the guards if they put him in with anybody else he'd be eating them for breakfast. But once they put him in there he took his mattress and put it up against his door so nobody could see in. This is against prison rules for visibility. So of course some guards had to go in there to take his mattress away. And as they did he told them when they came in that he'd be "servin' them up". Apparently he was true to his word and a couple of guards were seriously injured and never came back to work again. Where is the rehabilitation in prison and what are we lacking as a society to be allowing people like this to exist? We are obviously not helping all those in need because no one should be acting that way. What originally got Big Wick and Little Wick to end up in prison and why isn't the prison system working at trying to help them stop their violent behavior?

Little Wick's story about how he ended up in the hole is a little different. He was on a "maximum" security floor awaiting his trial. Somehow he had managed to smuggle an ounce of brown pot onto the floor. Its one thing if you have some open air. But anybody who knows MCC San Diego knows that you only get open air once a week on the top of the roof. In your unit, or on your floor its all enclosed so if you burn a joint or take a puff that smell will linger. I suppose a single hit here or there blown in the right vent though could go undetected. Thing of it was, Little Wick didn't have the brains to keep it on the down low and a guard came along and smelled something funny. Little Wick got freaked out and flushed his stash down the toilet just as the guard was walking into his cell. It must have totally reeked in there and the guard supposedly gave him the hardest of times even though there was no evidence. That was the first time. The second time this idiot got his stash smuggled in, he just straight away blew it by puffing out hard core during the day and was instantly busted and ended up punching a prison guard and going to the hole. Then he landed in some really horrible maximum security prison where nobody gets out alive. Prisons where dudes are getting dope smuggled into them and their shooting up right there in the yard and the guards don't care. Where dudes will be doin' dudes in their bed as guards walk by and they look the other way. Where you can puff a joint and talk on a cell phone if you're the right person and the guard won't say jack to you.

If its Atlanta USP, a particularly bad maximum security penitentiary, supposedly there's a female dental hygienist who will give it up for $500 worth of postage stamps, $100 for just her mouth. Who truly knows to what horrible depths humanity sinks too in those places on a daily basis. These are the kinds of places where when you don't get along with somebody you resolve it quick or one of you ends up getting killed. Its not like society where if you have a spat with somebody you can just walk away or get in your car and go home and hopefully never see them again. I think that is where mass transit has led to lack of accountability in our interpersonal relationships because if you have a fight with a family member it is too easy to get on a plane, or bus or car or train and go away and not deal with your problems. So things have a tendency to not get resolved. But in prison you have no place to go, except another prison maybe and that is a hard thing to have happen and doesn't happen quickly if it does at all.

Stories like Big and Little wick don't exactly make the case for a more compassionate approach to our nations problems. But the thing is, somewhere along the way somebody failed these people. Perhaps even many times. Who am I to say what has gone wrong, remember not any one of us can claim to have the whole answer. Only a part of it. And that's the part we have to contribute.

The hole. What a bad trip don't you think? Maybe there are some Hollywood movies out there about prison and so what. MTV has it's show the Land of Oz, but I don't think the general American public understands what it is really like. Not just the hole either. The whole prison construct we've set up. Not even the ones closest to the prison system, those who are in the justice system, they don't know either. The prosecutors or defense attorneys. None of them. All kinds of stories have been floating around that the BOP is cutting back its budget at a time prison populations are growing. 3% in 2002, 3% in 2003 and 3% in 2004. The great paradox with this is that somehow they have enough money to build new prisons, spending billions on their construction, and securing funding for their future staffing. And not only is there no oversight of their budget by anyone, no court nor congress, but nobody, not even the judges have jurisdiction over what transpires inside the prisons as I have said. Any television program that simulates such a preposterous proposition-that the BOP is managed and overseen is misleading you more than any street hustler ever did.

As long as we're talking about a hustle. Lets talk about how people are hustled out of their taxes every year and crunch some numbers on how that money gets spent at the border, during the judicial process and after sentencing.

The money spent at the border, as I have said, is hard to track. We'd have to go ask the different agencies how much they spend at the border and then combine the total. There is no point in asking them because, no matter what, the numbers you get from them wouldn't be accurate. Even if they "honestly" told you what they thought was the "truth", you still wouldn't have an accurate number. What is spent on the border is so huge, and at the same time not enough. The only reason is because of the way it is spent. When you break it down into salaried border agents, it can't compete with drug cartels and others who want to pay these agents huge bribes to look the other way.

After someone gets caught we can start tracking how much it costs the tax payers. All the numbers I am about to throw at you are from the Administrative Office of the United States Courts as of May 24, 2006. Keep in mind these are the numbers after years of budget reductions.

When somebody is caught trying to cross the border, be they white, black or Mexican, they are immediately housed by Customs and Immigration until they are processed and handed off to the Federal Marshals. What the cost to Customs and Immigration is nobody can be sure. But the second the Federal Marshals take them and put them in a detention center the Cost is $62.09 a day. So says the Administrative Office of the United States Courts. That's $1888.78 a month. This does not include transportation costs, or medical and dental expenses for the inmate while they are in custody. When you compare the pre trial detention costs of $62 a day to the amount it costs for somebody who gets out on bail, you may ask yourself why more people aren't let out on bail and why so many people are wrongfully denied bail. If the unlucky individual should get out on bail, the supervision by pre-trial services officers costs $5.7 a day, or $173.9 a month, compared to $1888.78. That's if you get out on bail while awaiting a trial. What the Administrative office didn't include was the cost of a trial, which if somebody asked for one it could cost anywhere from $40,000, for a short easy trial with almost no witnesses, to $100,000 and up for more lengthy complicated trials. It could top a million dollars and more if there are multiple defendants, multiple witnesses, multiple lawyers, multiple private investigators, multiple Federal Marshals, multiple everything which are needed to convict or exonerate them.

If they are convicted, which most are, trial or no trial, then off to prison they go where the daily cost goes up to $64.19 for average daily expenses. That's $1952.66 a month for one inmate. That does not include expenses related to transportation of inmates from one prison to the other. It does not include medical or dental costs. It does not include the cost of visitations by family or friends from the outside. Anything over and above the normal shuffling around of an inmate to and from meals, the meals themselves and counting the inmates is not included. It does not include the costs of sending somebody to the hole, or solitary. That is a huge expense right there. Just transferring someone to the hole requires no less than six prison guards and lots of guns.

Now you may say that sixty something dollars a day doesn't seem like a lot when considering the need to punish the guilty(or I should say, the sometimes guilty). But when you factor in medical costs and dental costs it skyrockets right off the charts. For most surgeries and operations of a technical nature the prison system ends up taking the inmate to a hospital close by the prison. The hospital doesn't have a special deal with the federal government. So the B.O.P. takes it on the chin and hard. Just a simple appendectomy costs $15,000. So any more complicated surgery just boosts that daily average expense of $64.19 through the roof. Now add dental and my guess is you are looking at anywhere from $150 to $200 a day, on the average. You may say how so? Or I don't believe you. Or how did you arrive at that number?

In the past, under Reagan, crazy prison sentences were being handed out based on all kinds of draconian laws requiring mandatory minimums and "three strikes your out" crimes. So guys back then were handed out 20, 30 and 40 year prison sentences. They walked in young men with no health problems. The trouble with having these kinds of sentencing guidelines is that inevitably your prison population is going to get old. Look out when it does because they are going to cost. Even though they may be prisoners, they are entitled to medical and dental care. The federal government has to pay for these services because it can't tell an inmate "well, we'll just wait on the appendectomy and see if your appendicitis gets any better." That would be a violation of the prisoner's rights. So for almost four decades the government spent almost a million dollars, average daily costs, on one individual and will fork over at least that much again to keep that prisoner "healthy." Each individual's medical needs are different, the costs vary from individual to individual. Imagine out there is an inmate that cost the B.O.P. a 10 million dollars in just medical expenses.

Then, assuming he or she survives their sentence, the inmate is thrown back out into society and set up for failure. After having grown old in prison they don't have the skills or energy to take on a full time job and meet all the requirements of the "post supervision," or their supervised release. In some districts the probation officers are just as ignorant as the prison guards are. Total average cost per day for supervised release? Supposedly $9.45 a day. Average. Throw in a drug test or a raid on an inmate's home for violating his probation, and that cost goes up too. The average cost of drug tests is about $20 in a retail store. The government has a slightly more sophisticated version, but because they probably get a good deal will just call their more sophisticated version $14 a drug test. On the average, (always on the average, wouldn't want to upset anybody over there at the GAO), an inmate out on supervised release gets drug tested 2 a month. Now some may only get tested 3 times, because their crime wasn't a drug crime. But an inmate out on supervised release who committed a drug crime gets drug tested once a week.

Before they get out on supervised release an inmate usually goes to what are commonly referred to as Community Corrections Centers for a couple of months. Again some stay longer than others depending on how long their prison sentence was. The longer the sentence the longer you stay in the CCC. They are also considered "halfway houses". Some of them are. The privately run ones.

No matter who is running them, they are a costly middle man back to society. Average daily cost at a Community Correction Center is $57.10 a day per inmate. The main function of these places is to make you get a job and then a place to stay and move you out. Before they do they will take money from both the Federal government and you. Since the "halfway" house is there to provide you with "resources" to reintegrate back into society, part of its mission is to make you start having the responsibilities of being back in society. This means that as soon as you get a job you have to start paying the halfway house rent out of your paycheck. So in addition to getting this daily fee from the B.O.P., they collect from you too! The majority of these halfway houses are run by private businesses. And they are definitely in it for the money. They churn inmates in and out of their facilities so fast. Sink or swim. If you don't get a job they don't want you there because you aren't paying them "rent" so they kick you back to prison to finish out your "good time" or "halfway" house time. If you swim then they collect some rent out of you for a couple of months, make sure you jump through all their hoops and then kick you out into the public.

From pretrial detention services and pretrial supervision services, depending on if you are stuck in jail without bail or out on bail and roaming the streets, to post trial imprisonment and then post imprisonment housing at a Community Corrections Center and then a probation officer, an inmate will have cost the taxpayers so much money. Money needlessly spent, money that should have been spent differently.

These things should be examined more closely by all of us as a collective consciousness to assess the efficacy of the prison and judicial systems. To assess whether we want them around anymore and in what capacity. I am sure the founding fathers never had this in mind when they created the Judicial branch. I seriously doubt they had anything in mind like the current prison system we have, the B.O.P. We all have to bear the social consequences and economic burden for having denied these people some help at some point along the way. The "well, they must have done something wrong in the first place to deserve being where they are right now," attitude just won't work anymore. Aside from which, that attitude displays the exact lack of compassion that the Christian dominated right wing keeps claiming it has. Yes, maybe these individuals in prison made some bad choices somewhere down the line. Does that mean they can't be redeemed? To deny them a chance because they screwed up once or twice only ensures that they'll screw up thrice. At which point it becomes a downward spiraling type of social determinism. Where society through its courts and prisons only affirm to the individual that he or she is no good. With so many people telling you that you are no good all the time, eventually you will end up being no good. That is the theory behind social determinism anyway.

Lets consider for a moment all this money. Instead of having spent it on all these prisons to further invalidate peoples' lives, what if we had just given it to these poor individuals who felt they could do nothing in life except break the law. After all we are talking about $23,431.92 a year for the average cost of imprisonment in the prison system. That's a lot of money to a poor person. Why take the risk? some would say. Why? Because if you spend that money on what I call the "front end" of society I predict only a small fraction of those given the money ever go back to crime. Anywhere you go you will find good and bad. Out of all those people you gave the money to only a small number would end up in prison. Why not spend this money in a positive way, making valid members of our society by economically empowering them to succeed. After all, isn't that what capitalism is all about? Amassing "principle" so you can "capitalize" on it. If that is the idea then right now as it stands capitalism is a dismal failure. The majority of people in the number one capitalist country in the world don't make enough to amass the necessary "principle" to be able to capitalize on it. So what is the point in participating? For the most part this is why people resort to crime.

In a pre-trial unit most people are just trying to hang in there. I am looking at a little bit of time, maybe two or three years at the most, so I am just trying to chill. Some are looking at a lot of time though so they don't care and would rather start making a name for themselves by picking fights. Mainly Mexicans, paisas, Border Brothers, Surenos, Nortenos and your random white dude going through MCC for some reason. To make a name for themselves they try to show others how tough they are by getting in fights. Its like a prison rite of passage. When you do get to where you are going, prison politics takes a drastic turn for the worse. In the detention centers it isn't so bad, but at medium and maximum security facilities there is a quest for control over the prison population that turns into out and out war sometimes. The different gangs of Mexicans and Central Americans like Mara Salvatrucha control the internal workings of the prison system by sheer numbers. When they fight, the prison officials send in guards in full riot gear with tear gas, guns and all. When that happens a whole prison will get locked down and somebody is going to the hole, if only to justify the expense of having all those guards in riot gear. Because the cost to put all those guards in riot gear is double your normal cost. Just to suit up in riot gear the guards get what is called hazard pay for the day. When that happens the warden becomes the second most powerful person in that state of the union the prison happens to be in. This is because, at the warden's discretion, he can order the governor to call out the National Guard to assist with quelling a prison riot. In fact there is something else the warden can do should things get really bad on the outside of the prison: it has to do with FEMA regulations, and we all know how awesome FEMA has been lately.

***

Should a war ever reach our soil, supposedly part of FEMA national emergency procedures is to gas all federal inmates to death right away, right where they are. The way the prisons have been built nobody needs to be taken to a "gas chamber". Its all built in and part of the design specifications of each prison. The fire sprinkler systems within each and every prison have been built for a dual purpose. All the water can be flushed out if need be and filled up again with your choice of deadly nerve gas and turned on. So if a war hits this country's shores all federal inmates will be exterminated like rats.

The "rationale" behind this emergency plan is to make sure none of these bad guys gets out and joins the invading forces. It frees up the guards to go back to active combat duty. It is also so that the government has one less segment of the population to worry about, a segment that is unwanted during a time of war. These arguments are so neat and convenient but they all point back to one type of thought emanating from the government and those controlling us from within it. The thought is called fascism. We might as well gas all the homeless while we are at it because they would also be very likely to join an invading force. How many homeless are there in this country?

Might as well gas minimum wage earners too, they'll be likely to join the invading forces in the hopes of a better life under a new regime. Silly me, I am sure the government already has a plan in pace to do that. While we're at it lets round up any suspicious characters who look like they might have thoughts that don't coincide with current policy(and we'll look the other way when racial profiling happens because after all, "better safe than sorry").

If they wanted to kill the prisoners they wouldn't need to do much. Each unit has two gas masks which are in the guards' station. There is such a lack of guards that there are seldom more than two at any given time on any given floor at MCC and throughout the prison system. If the word came from FEMA, all the guards would have to do was make sure everyone was locked down. Most of the time we don't know why we are getting locked down, so it could be just a count or something. So we all just go peacefully when they call lockdown. Then the guard simply goes to his station, closes the door for extra security, puts the mask on, waits for the gas to be released from the sprinkler system and watches us all die like rats and then leaves and goes about his business of living the rest of his life.

Most people in our society don't know about all these wonderful plans the government has to protect the people should things get "bad." Every time there was a lockdown I thought about what if it were the last lockdown and sometimes I'd look to see if they were putting the masks on. After all we are at war, and by definition war had come to our shores- the War on Terror started with 9/11, and the government has come up with all kinds of crazy "definitions" in the past about what a war is. So it would be no surprise if they looked at it as "war reaching our shores" and redefining it to suit their needs at some opportune moment in the future (but they would have to be really sure because with all the inmates dead, then all those prisons wouldn't be needed anymore). Lockdowns and their ramifications, were enough for me to want to get the hell out of there as quickly as possible.

These fears come into play every day whether we want to admit it or not. Across the Bureau of Prisons men live with secret personal fears of all kinds of things. Most will never admit it. They'd like you to think their tough. Some of them are. The rest are just regular men with normal fears, insecurities, and preoccupations. They worry about their families on the outside. They worry for their own safety on the inside. Some of their fears are abnormal or irrational and some aren't. Sometimes fear can be a healthy response to a situation. A doctor being afraid to make a mistake in an operation can be a good thing. Chances are he'll be more careful out of fear of malpractice lawsuits against him. A prisoner's fears can be a tool for redemption. Sometimes redemption happens instantly without the need for fear. Sometimes redemption can't happen.

I speak of redemption rather than rehabilitation because I don't believe the word or concept of rehabilitation fully covers what needs to happen to make people feel better about themselves in order to live life without hurting others. When somebody does something wrong they know on some level that they did something wrong. When they are punished they become acutely aware of it, for better or for worse. Sometimes they will resist the punishment by tricking themselves into believing they shouldn't be punished. They develop this kind of self-righteous anger and indignation at having been punished. It is almost as if they had forgotten that they committed a wrong in the first place.

It is only through their own personal acceptance of what they did and the realization that what they did was bad that redemption can begin to take place. Certainly somebody who shows no remorse for the bad they've done in life is not somebody redeemed. But somebody who knows the good and bad, right and wrong, through their own good and bad deeds, is in a better position to determine the difference between the two. A better position than somebody who supposedly has never done any wrong in life.

The strange thing is that our society doesn't really believe in redemption even though the vast majority are Christian. They believe in Jesus, but won't hear his true message. He even said they would not. Not a hard one to figure out considering the types of people who go spewing forth Christian litanies without thinking if their own actions are in accordance with their principles. I believe there are some men in prison who are more in touch with the spirit than people on the outside who go to church every week. Those inmates redeemed themselves long ago behind bars. Long ago.

Jose had been caught trying to smuggle cocaine into the country. The government gave him a 10 year sentence. His prison sentence is the very thing which saved his life. But not because bible thumpers came to him and converted him. Jesus talks about it. Its called your own personal salvation. If people would just concern themselves with saving themselves maybe the world would be a better place.

I say it saved him because quite literally it did. When he came into prison he was a very sick man. He didn't know it until they had him go for his physical with the doctor. They took his blood and urine and gave him a routine physical. In prison they want to know right away if you have an infectious disease so they can determine where to place you. Not that they always place you in a way that makes sense anyway but if you have tuberculosis then they want you on medication right away and might quarantine you until it takes effect. If you have AIDS they will try to find you a cellmate or bunkmate who also does. If you have Hepatitis C they want to give you meds to control it.

Jose had Hepatitis C. Hep C, a supposedly incurable disease that can kill you. Jose went about his business until one day not too long after he was imprisoned he found a book on mantras and meditations. So he meditated and as he told me, was given a mantra out of the ether to repeat for himself. So he did. Along with his mantra he repeated another mantra. A very curious one he would repeat while urinating. It went like this "The Hep c is leaving this body. The Hep c is leaving this body." And for about two years Jose repeated these mantras until one day he was called to medical for a regular check up to see how things were going with his Hep c.

I wish I could have seen the look on those doctors faces when the results came back. I bet one rubbed his eyes as if to clear them so he could see the "truth." It was a miracle. At least it should have been declared a miracle. The media should have been called. It should have been on the front page of the local newspaper. It should have been front page across the nation!

Instead, for the BOP, it was an excuse to call in the psyche doctors. Because when the prison officials found out what he was telling them about how he had cured himself, they freaked out. Because it was a self healing through faith in something other than Jesus so it had to be…..well….crazy. Right? So they brought in psyche doctors to debunk his story and in any way possible invalidate him so nobody would ever hear that it is possible to have a non-Christian miracle in this world. The funny thing is these prison officials had their own evidence. Their own blood and urine tests. If what he was saying wasn't true then how else had it happened? Having the evidence and still refusing to see the light is also something our society is really good at doing and the enormous cost to all of us because of this "refusing to see the light" is mounting daily.

Jose's redemption came with the curing of an incurable disease through the purification and cleansing of mind, body and soul through meditation and mantra repetition. Redemption in prison takes place in other forms as well. Some of them are instantaneous. For some, just a teardrop from the most dreaded toughest inmate is all it takes.

If our courts only had a way to see who has really found redemption, then prison overcrowding wouldn't be happening. I met some men who were totally repentant of what they had done to land them in prison. If you can see who has achieved redemption but you persist on punishing them who is worse? A man who has redeemed himself in the first year of prison doesn't need the rest of a 20 year prison sentence. Society doesn't need to pay for it either. I think that was also part of Jesus' message if I'm not wrong. Just like the Sadducees and Pharisees were living by the letter of the law and not by the spirit, the government is making all kinds of people suffer as a result of their reckless and arbitrary application of the law without any thought or care given to a higher law of conduct that has been a part of man's existence through all religions and ages. A law of conduct that "bad" men may understand better than "good" men, the concept of the hard right over the easy wrong. Maybe the prison situation isn't so much for the redemption of the errant individual, but for the errant society as a whole. Through redoing our laws and reviewing our prisons we can all learn some lessons about redemption. These lessons don't come easy and can't be learned in a group or class. These are all lessons learned individually. Our personal redemption.

Who am I to say? Somebody would point the finger at me and say "who are you to talk to us of morals and ethics? You are a convicted felon. Why should we listen to you? Who cares about your life?"

These are heavy issues to be thinking about and most of us never get through them. Most of us never think about them in the first place. After all, its just a bunch of bad guys in prison. Who cares what they may complain about, right? They're bad guys!

But I am thinking about these thoughts of redemption on my last day in MCC. I'm sure I'll never come back here. Once I post bail I'm gone. But for the next couple of hours I have to endure the mindless world of prison. The guards, the inmates the bathrooms, the food and the random lockdowns.

Speaking of lockdowns, they just called for a count which means we all go back to our ranges and stand by our bunks waiting for two guards to come around and count us all. Must be they think somebody escaped. How they think somebody did that I don't know. This building is so secure its not possible in my mind. But hey what do I know.

Normally they have a morning, an afternoon and three evening counts during the night. The reason for two guards is because they don't want guards helping prisoners to escape or miscounting afterwards. More often than not these geniuses can't count straight anyway, end up with different numbers, and have to do a recount which means we are locked down for longer while they get it straightened out.

We all start moving to our ranges. Some are getting a last dash of hot water for their coffees or ice for their Tangs. I just go straight back to my bunk. Morale is pretty low today. They all know I'm almost out of here. Funny how they are sad at my good fortune on getting out of here. That's just the human condition though; we're happy when others are sad and sad when others are happy. I don't ascribe to that, but it seems like so many others do. A common way of acting towards someone more impoverished or of a different race than the "morally right" of the United States is to kick a down and out person in the face instead of help them. Anytime somebody is hurting in the community instead of helping them get out of the dumps the community actually just tries to shit on them harder and run them out of town. I don't know how many times I've heard it and seen it. Seems like it happens more in small town U.S.A. Very Christian like of those small town people. I guess it has to do with something like feeling good about your lot in life no matter how bad it is because at least there is always somebody else who is worse off than you are who you can kick in the face. Oh well.

You can just feel the depression here. Its understandable. I have been a ray of hope and happiness in an otherwise dismal place. John is sitting on his bunk, legs crossed, chin touching his chest; snoozing. I usually find him like that. Doesn't matter what time of day it is. Being 70 and waiting for trial without bail is like a death sentence all unto itself.

Pops is there too. But never sleeping. He's sitting on the edge of his bed wringing his hands, one over the other. I wonder if he thinks that helps make the time go faster. He laughs a lot and worries more. Its amazing how white people feel here. They are so worried somebody is going to hurt them. But what they don't realize is that the Mexicans are just as worried about that and never getting home again.

Indio's just lying down in his corner bunk looking out his tiny little slit of a window at San Diego bay and watching all the Navy ships. The mafia gun salesman guy on the bunk above him is lying down, eyes closed.

Poor Chuck. He is one angry man. He's told us how he hates just about everybody. Jews, Blacks and Mexicans especially. At one point I had to tell him to keep his mouth shut or he'd get it shut for him. He wanted to know if I'd be doing that. I told him yeah and called over this little Mexican dude named Jairo.

Jairo was a short man built to the max. An ex flyweight boxer in Tijuana, he had tried his best to find other work there but had had no luck. So I asked Chuck if he wanted to repeat what he had said and no words came out. End of story for Chuck, a sick old white man caught in the councilman scandal and the porno strip bar mobster scandal. If he makes it to the "pen" as it is called, word will reach somebody there and he'll be dead within the year. His story is a sad and twisted tale of hatred and violence.

The story about the Jairo is very interesting indeed. His boxing days were long since over. This little guy had tried for years after to find work in his own country that would provide for his wife and little girl. He never did find anything that he could do to make ends meet in Tijuana simply because there isn't anything to do in Tijuana to make ends meet unless you are already rich or willing to work for the mob. The sole reason Tijuana exists is because of the border. In fact the sole reason any of these border towns like Nogales or Nuevo Laredo or Cuidad Juarez exist is because of all the illegal border money. If you go to any one of those towns and see all the shops for souvenirs for sale you'd ask yourself; who buys this junk and how do these shops stay open even? The answer is that almost all of those shops are a front for something else going on at the border, something else that is illegal. Even the border crossings themselves are purely there for money.

I was in Nogales once. I had just hitchhiked from Southern Mexico and was waiting there to meet my wife who was supposed to come down and pick me up. My hitching was so successful I was early by a day. While waiting, a guy approached me who they simply called "El Tio Politico". This name means he is like a mob boss or something. He asked me if I had a passport and driver's license. I told him I did and he then asked me if I wanted to make a lot of money driving a truck to Vegas. I asked him what the deal was. So he told me there would be a couple of hundred pounds of marijuana strapped to the undercarriage of the car. I asked him what would happen if I got stopped at the border crossing and busted. He laughed and said not to worry. If he gave the word "the red truck gets through lane 7 at 3 o'clock any day of the week.

That means that a border agent must be on the take, but more importantly, more than one agent must be on the take to be able to say "seven days a week."

There are so many stories like that. So many. After you start seeing and hearing about more and more "isolated" incidents of corruption you start to ask; when does it stop being isolated and start becoming a pandemic? No amount of fences are going to keep drugs or people out so long as border agents are on the take at the border crossings themselves. The National Guard can't stay on the border forever. They might be called out to invade Iran (I recently talked to somebody on leave from an Army base that they are making preparations to do that right now.)

The fact of the matter is border agents' salaries are so piddly and the bribe money being offered to look the other way is too great for them to say no. They are humans after all, capable of making "bad" decisions. But you never see Border agents getting caught and going to prison.

So because Jairo couldn't make it work on three dollars a day for him and his family in Tijuana he started jumping the border. The first time he made it to L.A. and got a job working in a welding shop. For a while he was able to provide for his family. He lived in a two bedroom apartment in Compton with six other men. All of them sent their money home to their families. Using fake social security numbers they paid taxes into somebody's account and never got them back because they were sure they could never file taxes and get them back. So the IRS got to keep their money, like it keeps the money of millions of others who never file a return each year after they spent the whole year paying into a system that considered them "shadow workers." The IRS probably keeps about 50 billion in unclaimed taxes every year and never tells a soul. What it does with that money we will never know because there is no law which forces them to disclose that information. Kind of like the B.O.P.'s budget.

Meanwhile Jairo is busy pursuing the American dream. He's paying taxes, sending money back to his family and everything is going great until Immigration raids his work and deports him. He crosses over again after a brief bittersweet reunion with his wife and child. By now they have become accustomed to being apart for long stretches and have resigned themselves to it as the only way to survive. They know they have no chance at a better life together in Tijuana. Apart, they just might be able to live o.k. As a father he has realized the only way to provide for his daughter is to do this thing he is not supposed to do.

The second time you get caught crossing the border its six months. So he had done six months at MCC already. As he told me: " Look man, I am not afraid to cross the border. First of all God gave this land to the Mexicans first. You Gringos scammed it from us. Second, I'm not afraid of crossing the border because if I make it I go to L.A. and get a good job homey. If I get caught, well I stay at MCC like the last time and work in the welding shop here and make three bucks an hour homey and I send all that home to my woman and its enough for her and my little girl to live on.. That is way more than in Tijuana. Plus I get free clothes, free food and shelter. Best of all homey, the medical care here is better than what I'd get in Tijuana. Not only that homey, but if I get to L.A. somebody may scam me or maybe I get weak and drink or something. If I'm here then I am safe from that temptation homey. And if everything go ok in L.A. maybe after I pay for food and rent and all that I have only three dollars an hour left or less to send home to her. So its better for me to be here. Either way I still can't go back to see my wife and girl. So it don't matter homey"

He's looking at a year and a half here at MCC then re-lease back to Tijuana. Except maybe he won't be sent back to Tijuana. Our wonderful government has devised a plan (or so it thinks) to keep the same individuals from coming back in so many times. When it sends you back to Mexico, if you're from Tijuana, they'll fly you to Cancun or Mexico City and leave you there without a dime to your name. How in the world as a poor person are you supposed to reunite with your family? If you are from Mexico City they'll send you somewhere else. Just to mess with you. But hey you should be punished for trying to come to this land of the free and the cowardly George Bushes. This land comprised of total immigrants (except for the people who were here before Columbus arrived.) So at least for a year and a half he'll be able to provide for his family, get free food, clothes, dental work and a place to stay all courtesy of the U.S. taxpayer, instead of allowing him to become a valid member of the community and pay taxes himself. Oh yeah, forgot, that's not supposed to happen because if it did he might file a return and actually get his taxes back from the IRS. They don't want that.

There are others like Jairo too. He's not the only one. And no matter what story they have, even if the details are different, they are all the same and tell the tale of individuals left behind. This other guy, we called him Taliban sometimes, other times we called him Chuck Norris, his story is even more messed up. He's this little dude who had arrived recently. He had this beard like Chuck Norris or a Taliban or something like that, but his body was small and thin. He had bad scars and blemishes all over his skin. He's definitely got something wrong with him. Both physically and mentally. The mental part we got right away when he told us how glad he was to be here with all of us. He was a street person from Tijuana. He told us he looked forward to Fall because that was his cue to cross and try to make it to L.A. If he made it, as he had in past years, he would sell his body to gay men. This is a 30 year old man. A street person who more than likely carries more than one sexually transmitted disease. And if he didn't make it and got caught, then he was glad to be in prison because there was lots of men there to make money off of. Either way it didn't matter to him.

He didn't last long. One night we found him walking around while everybody was sleeping. Looking at people, touching some. Next morning we rolled him up and he was gone to the thunderous roar of "HILO". Moved to another floor or to the psyche ward. Things should change so that communicable diseases are kept under control better. Since these are just "throw away" individuals nothing will be done and the situation will get worse with AIDS and other diseases.

Speaking of STDs, we had a rather amusing incident happen here in our range not too long ago. When I first came in and was processed I was on the fourth floor where everybody goes before they are assigned to a different floor. Its like a way station to the rest of the prison. And we were all dressed in white jumpsuits so when we got to our floor everybody knew we were new. The day I was leaving that floor we were called out to eat lunch and I walked by this cell where I heard this man crying. I walked up to the door and looked in and saw a young Mexican crying. He was white, not your darker skin. In Mexico they have whites, they call them gueros. Anyway this guy was from a really big drug running Mexican gang (supposedly, and I believe it for reasons I will not say in the book) but he was younger and more tender so to speak. He had been busted with 2 kilos of cocaine and his wife and kid were all the way back in Sinaloa. We'll just call him Chinola, the nickname they give to people from there. Anyway, he had had a good job and somebody in his clan had come and taken it away from him and told him he had to do this drug running thing.

Well, when he first got caught and was on the fourth floor crying there I went into his cell and told him not to worry, everything was going to be ok. When he told me a little of his story I told him mine, about my pregnant wife and little boy and it cheered him up, and he came out and had lunch with me.

Later, on the Seventh floor he was put in the same range as me and we became friends. I started teaching him English, and since he had a lot of money, he bought me a flashlight to read at night with and he lent me his radio so I could rock out sometimes.

Apparently before he tried to cross the border he had slept with a hooker. This was one of the reasons he had been crying that day on the fourth floor, because his last sex before he got caught wasn't even with his own wife but some hooker out of Ensenada. He didn't find out until a month later that she had given him crabs. The crabs had spread to the other inmates around his bunk. Once he realized it he came to me because he didn't trust anybody else to tell this horrible thing to and he needed to get some help from the medical people (which was always a scary thing in and of itself). Quite often I found myself translating between the guards and the Mexicans. This time Chinola needed me to help him.

He had brought me a cup covered with a piece of cardboard. He opened it up a little and this huge crab tried to jump out. I jumped back. I realized instantly and ran to the gate and yelled for the guard, even though it was ten at night. The guard finally came over and wanted to know what all the hubbub was about. When I showed him the cup and its contents he jumped back.

It took an hour before the Medical people (I say "medical people" because seldom was a doctor around and often we wondered what qualified these people to be working as, well, medical people) came and took Chinola and all his clothes and bedding and three other inmates to a quarantine area. There they were taken care of. In the meantime these fraidy cat white guys were all swearing to the high heaven that if they got crabs there would be trouble. I told them all to pipe down. Then Curly and I got together and had a good laugh because we had just come up with the new moniker for the prison. MCC: My Criminal Crab. We laughed so hard tears came to our eyes and everybody else got upset with us for making so much noise at one in the morning.

Those medical people were lame. They made the guards turn on all the lights and they made the guards go into the range with gloves on and carry out all the stuff that could have been contaminated. Anytime you ask a guard to do something like that he is going to take his sweet time with it and make everybody suffer through it. And so it wasn't until 12:30 a.m. that things started getting back to normal all because some guys had some crabs. That's when Curly and I were amped after all the commotion. We all finally got to sleep that night but from then on MCC took on a little bit lighter meaning for us because at least we hadn't got crabs and we were all able to laugh about MCC's new name.

Waiting for the count. That's what prison was all about; multiple counts every day. And your day and time were broken up by them. They didn't make things go faster or slower. They were just like punctuation marks in a book. Today's emergency count was brought to you by a suicide and a gang fight on floor 8, so the gossip mill had us believe. How these rumors got started I never understood, but more importantly how they were believed by these people I really never understood. All these grown men, stressed out and acting like little school girls for all intensive purposes. Really. Like the television. All these men would fight for control of the television only to put on programming they wouldn't be caught dead watching if they were on the outside. Not only wouldn't they be caught dead watching those programs, but they would probably ride others hard for watching them. Programs like soap operas and cheesy celeb programs and reality shows. Lately its been non-stop Arnold Schwarzenegger movies. We are convinced he bought the airwaves for the last month leading up to his election for governor so he could be guaranteed a win. The movies repeated too, on the same channels night and day. All these bozos just sitting around and watching them again and again. Terminator was played more in the last month on television than at any other time since it first started airing on television years ago. I came up with a great idea for it. He should make another Terminator movie and call it Terminator Four: the Death of California. What a punk. If he thinks he fooled us he's wrong. We know he and his snobby ass bride rigged those elections. He will unravel with time and be gone before you know it.

"Walking," some inmate says. That means the guards have come to count and its your cue to stand up next to your bunk as they walk through. They call them "stand up counts". If you are not standing up you had better be really sick or dead because if the guards come around and you are not standing they will take you to the hole. One time I stood up, on my head, as they walked by. They asked me what the fuck I thought I was doing. And I told them.

"Didn't see anywhere in the prison rules where it said I had to be standing on my feet or that I couldn't be standing on my head. It just said standing so that is what I am doing." They didn't do anything to me. The others were shocked.

This time its two guards we have come to call Popeye and the Pillsbury doughboy. Seriously that is what they look like. Their body types and faces will have repeated themselves as if they had been cloned many times during my entire prison stay in the federal system before I finally get out once and for all. They come through quick, do their thing and are gone. At least they know how to count. Popeye is from Massachusetts I could tell right away when I first heard him speak. One time he called us all losers for being here and so I had to chime in. Ex-military himself and an ex-border agent (as we found out from him at one point) I had to challenge him. So I said, "mind if I say something?"

"No. Not at all," he said, not knowing what he was getting himself into. Most of these prison guards cop an attitude of superiority here because they think all the prisoners are just a bunch of uneducated, non-English speaking wetbacks. So when they come across somebody like me who can actually outwit them and beat them down intellectually they eventually stay away from because to hear your thoughts would actually rock their world so hard they wouldn't be able to go on living the way they do and still feel ok with it.

Its called the Karmic Adjustment. I love doing it, no matter what may happen to me. It's my mission in life. I feel the need to adjust people's minds and realities so they stop being shits. Even if they hate me the rest of their lives, I don't care so long as they swallowed the adjustment.

"I think you are the real loser, You are here because you are ex military who couldn't get a real job with a reputable corporation (little does he know I actually think the words reputable and corporation in the same sentence as a compound noun constitute an oxymoron) for the life of you. Nobody would hire you so you are stuck working this job risking getting AIDS and Hepatitis C and who knows what else. And for how much a month? And, what's next after this? You have very limited options for career advancement. One injury or accident and you are off to take a pay cut as some security guard in an office building. Whoop di fukin' do for you. Think about what you are doing here. Are you really accomplishing much? You're fighting a losing battle against immigration and drugs at best and at worst you are fighting a losing battle against your own government which is secretly involved in letting these drugs and people across the border unhampered."

"What do you mean?" he asked

"Well, how in the world do you think so much drugs gets across the border undetected? Do you think its me or some other individual supplying L.A.'s coke habit for example? No the drug market and need is too big to be supplied by a bunch of small timers bringing in a kilo at a time. Look," I said, "If Cuban cigars are illegal and you can't find a one, well, maybe you could find one if you knew the right people and you waited a day or two, but how in the world do explain all these trucks of coke making it into the country every day when not a single Cuban cigar can get across? Don't you think the U.S. Government is in on it? I mean this Border is a money maker. The government isn't about to stop the flow of drugs or illegals into this country. Cuban cigars are also not so lucrative its true, but this country needs undocumented workers. It's the Republican business owners who use them as modern day slaves. They set up substandard housing, have company stores nearby that charge way to much for their goods and they pay misery wages. So of course they don't want them here legally because then they'd actually have to treat them like human beings and give them a decent wage.

So those same Republicans lobby congress for stiff immigration policies and anti citizen laws. And drugs keep the people downtrodden, unfocused and poor so they can't pay attention to what the government is secretly doing behind their backs. So its to the governments' advantage to let drugs in. Plus, education spending, which started its decline during the Nixon era, because they thought people were too educated and that was why they were protesting the Vietnam war, is at an all time low. This government doesn't want smart educated people who would be likely to stand up against the atrocities of this administration. Illegals? Well, if they weren't here you'd have no fruit or vegetables to eat. So why don't you go hungry then loser if your so against illegals. And the level of corruption at the border is so high how much longer do you think the government can hide it?

"Do you know what the only difference between this country and Mexico is?"

"No what?" he retorted.

"The only difference is that in Mexico at least they aren't in denial and they openly admit that their government is the mafia. Here we still think somehow our government isn't corrupt or bought off. So if you are so against drugs why don't you go bust the largest drug dealers in this country I can tell you where they are right now."

"Where are they?" he naively asked.

"They are in Texas and their names are George Bush senior and George Bush Junior so go get them and throw them in jail Dudley do right." Huge guffaws of laughter peel through the range from those listening in who could understand.

"You're crazy," he said.

"I am? Where the hell were you during the Iran Contra scandal? Or had you forgotten about that? And the BCCI scandal out of Karachi Pakistan. You know, the Bank of Commerce and Credit International? The bank the CIA used to pay Osama bin Laden in the 1980's. The bank used to buy large quantities of heroin and used for cash transfers for the sale of U.S. military equipment. Go read the transcripts on either of those scandals if you dare to find out the truth about guns for drugs for money and who was in on it and when. Why do you think the Bushes moved to Texas? So they could be closer to the border and manage their corrupt empire better and bring the drugs and illegals in easier with all the corrupt people they could marshal together. The Bush family is one of if not the largest drug dealing family in the world. They are the axis of evil, George, Jeb and George Jr. The border is rampant with corruption man. Jeb and George junior controlled Florida and Texas borders, you think they don't have their hands in the pie? That's where most of the cocaine gets in the country is from those two states. Miami Vice man. Come on open your eyes and admit you are on the wrong side. "

"I was a border agent," he said "and I know those are isolated incidents." I laughed so hard when he said that it made snot blow out my nose. A couple of the others chuckled at this. I wiped the snot away with my jumpsuit before I continued on with my adjustment.

"Isolated incidents? Isolated incidents? Let me ask you, how many isolated incidents do you need to have before you have a pattern bordering on epidemic proportions? How about the seven FBI agents in Massachusetts that went down for drug corruption? Why don't you open your eyes and do a little investigating. Come on , you know this government is corrupt from the top down. I know you can't admit it here but spare us your pathetic patriotic drivel. You're not going to get us to believe it. Hell some of the people here on this floor probably know different first hand because they themselves have given money to corrupt border agents, cops, lawyers and maybe even judges."

"Judges? right," he said as if he could sow doubt in my mind.

"Of course judges too. You think they aren't human? You think they aren't capable of having a weak moment and giving in to temptation and corruption."

"Name one." he challenged.

"Come on now, you think I am stupid enough to sign my own death certificate? If I knew I wouldn't tell you, could be the judge who gets me off and if I tell you I'm just shit out of luck for being stupid enough to tell the enemy and get that judge in my pocket busted before he gets me off.

" But I'll tell you this, prove to me that all these things aren't going on. You have no evidence to prove your argument, but I have reams of newspapers saved at my home which shows I'm right and millions of illegals here working keeping America strong and literally tons of drugs being sold on the streets. How about that CIA agent who got off the plane in Amarillo Texas with a signed document from Bushy Sr. giving him permission to bring a plane load of cocaine into this country. That was in the New York Times. You know what happened to him don't you?"

He just shook his head.

"He was met by law enforcement and media. They took him away to a federal detention center like this one. It was in the New York Times man, like on the front page when it happened back in 1989. I remember. And then a couple days later on like page 19 a little article appeared about how he and his evidence had somehow been misplaced or disappeared. Now when you are innocent, as I am assuming Bushy Sr. was, you'd think they'd be darn sure to keep that boy under lock and key to make sure he was proven wrong. But when you are guilty and you don't want anybody knowing, especially the wife you've lied to for years, then you make sure the guy disappears along with all his documents and evidence against you so he can never tell his story again. What do you think about that?"

"Don't talk to me anymore," he said.

"Don't worry, I won't, wouldn't want to totally break you out of your bubble and cause you to have a psychological break down." And I walked away. Ever since then Popeye never spoke to me. I wasn't your typical downtrodden white guy or non-Eng-

lish speaking Mexican he could manhandle in a debate. After
that Curly came up to me and told me to watch out and that I
shouldn't take on the guards like that because they could take
me to the hole. I laughed.

It was still early and I was wondering if I'd ever get to court
to take care of my bail today. It was almost getting to be too late
for them to call me out to go to court. Especially with an emergency count happening. These Federal assholes were so lazy. All
the way through the system right to the very courtroom itself. If
I didn't have a birth to get to, namely that of my second son, I
wouldn't care. But I knew my time was getting close to needing
to be leaving here.

After count Curly and Chicharron came up to talk with
me. Chicharron is the word for pork rind in Spanish. The reason
they called him that was because when he shaved his head his
neck and head looked like a chicharron. He could move his head
in a certain way and the back of his neck would scrunch up and
look like a pork rind. I swear.

"Hey," Curly started to say, "me and Chicharron need to
talk with you about something."

"Oh yeah?" I said. "What's up?" It was a strange combo.
Biker dude and Sureno wanting to team up on something?
Couldn't be good. It was then they told me about this guy named
Jay-Lo who was over in the Wackenhut detention center. A man
who it just so happens had ratted them both out on separate
occasions.

Wackenhut. Now that is a scary word. Who in the world
came up with that name? Whoever it was, curse him and his family. Wackenhut is the agency that originally started contracting
with the Federal government to secure Roswell, New Mexico after the U.F.O. crashed there. If you travel through New Mexico

today there are more "areas", not just Area 51. There are areas 1 through 51, and all of them off limits to the public and all of them protected by the Federal Government's contractor, Wackenhut.

To make things even more sinister, Wackenhut now contracts with the Federal government to provide prison services. It also contracts with our wonderful government to provide protective services to the public in places like Portland, Oregon. There the focus is on the transit malls. You'd think what does a federal contractor have to do with mass transit? Well, it just so happens that the mass transit in Portland and the surrounding area is funded in part by federal tax dollars which allows the federal government to bully its local and state counterparts to accept Wackenhut as its security detail. What is really scary is that they, in addition to the local police, county sheriffs and state troopers, also carry guns. To the untrained eye or just the simple unobservant nincompoop the militarization of our country goes unnoticed. Local, County, and State cops. FBI, CIA, DEA, ATF, NSA, Federal Protective Services (still can't figure out when that came about) Forest Service Rangers, Federal Marshals and Homeland Security. The government and the media do such a good job at boondoggling the public about it that a person like me who would seek to draw attention to such anomalies in the law enforcement system is labeled a conspiracy theorist. The reality of it is that it is no longer a theory when you have facts and can connect the dots. At that point I become a conspiracy realist.

Right now though I've got Curly and Chicharron telling me about this guy named Jay-Lo who apparently is being housed "across the street" at the Wackenhut facility. When I go to court, which should be in minutes, they want me to pass a message along to any surenos or paisas being housed at Wackenhut that they will pay to have Jay-Lo hospitalized. All I need to do is pass the message along and all the rest will get taken care of according to them. See, I had questions about how they will find out who did the deed and who gets the money and how they are going to get it to them. But I forget, I am in Federal Prison and anything is possible here just like it is on the outside. All it takes is a little more "juice" to get it done, that's all. "Juice", what a good term for it. Don't say words like "power" here. This is the pre-trial unit and it is quite possible there are secret microphones around. I doubt it, but others don't. If you think I am a conspiracy theorist, talk to my bunkie John. He makes me look tame. And Curly and Chicharron? The whole of their conversation with me about this was either written on a piece of paper to be thrown away afterwards, flushed down the toilet, or they whispered in the softest of tones what they needed to tell me. When it comes to harming another inmate you don't want a trail leading back to you. Not unless you want to do more time. Some people don't care because they are already looking at life or some really long prison sentence, like the guy who killed that gay priest in Massachusetts. He was proud of what he did. The guys who killed Jeffrey Dahlmer, wow what a job they did on him. They stuck a broom stick up his ass until it came out his stomach. He died of course. And in his case I think the guards must have looked the other way because whoever did that never got caught. And you know what? It's called "prison justice" and it happens every day and only when our society at large doesn't fulfill its obligations judiciously. O.J., wherever you are, I hope a group of radical lesbians get you!

Larios, a guard, comes to open our gates and we are "free" again to wander around the unit. Larios is a funny guy. Out of all the prison guards I have to say I like his style. He's tough but has a streak of compassion in him. In the morning he reads his paper and when he is done he gives it to me. He told me he wanted to give it to me because he knew I'd be fair about passing it around and knew that I'd read some of the articles out loud in Spanish for the non-English speakers. He also asked me at one point to help him. Imagine that, me help him. He wanted help with Yoga. He had seen me doing yoga and heard I was a yoga teacher. He wanted to impress his girlfriend who is into yoga. So I wrote out three whole pages of instructions for him. He was very thankful. Talk about redemption in the strangest of places. Here's a prison guard asking an inmate for spiritual guidance without even knowing.

I make another coffee knowing that as soon as I do my name will be called out. Murphy's law. And sure enough, as I am taking my first sips my name is called out and off I go.

The first step in this process of going to the courthouse is getting patted down before I leave the unit. They do not want you taking any written messages to your attorney so they check any and all paperwork you may be carrying. I am carrying nothing. No need. I am out of here within hours of now anyway.

The next step in this whole draconian process is going down in the elevator to the depths of the building to be shackled to all the other pre-trialers. Bound to each other hand and foot. While we wait for the doors to open we face the wall and look down. We are patted down a second time. Then the door opens and we shuffle through to a long corridor underneath the street. MCC and the Federal courthouse are across the street from each other and so the corridor, though it seems long, isn't more than a hundred yards. It's a hundred yards with so much high-tech cameras and security devices it makes you wonder why these people are so afraid.

We get to the other side and another door opens and we walk up a flight of stairs. We are led to the right and told to face the wall again. This time a female federal marshal with latex gloves on pats us down and as we are patted down one by one, we are released from our shackles and directed to one of several holding cells.

The holding cells are designed to hold up to fifty men and the one they put me in is almost full. There are three different kinds of jumpsuits being worn that I can see. The yellow of MCC, the green of Wackenhut and orange from where I can't remember and don't care. My focus is to find a green suit I can talk to. And I do. This one very sophisticated looking Mexican with John Lennon style glasses is quietly sitting minding his own business. So I take a chance and sit next to him.

"Hey man, I got a message for you from a sureno named Chicharron from Calexico."

"Ain't you a whitey homey?"

"Yeah, but don't matter sureno, el Chicharron me dijo que buscara otro sureno o paisa para darle un mensaje."

"Adelante cavron. A ver."

So I tell him the whole story (which I will not tell in this book) and his eyes light up with understanding.

"Yeah, we know who that rat is and you can tell Chicharron and the biker dude that we already took care of it and no need to send anybody any money. A rat's a rat and gets taken care of like a rat. Tell 'em job done homey. We already broke his ass off and he's in hospital."

"Ok man, that will be music to their ears."

"I'm Lomas homey. What they get you with?" He had it tattooed all the way down his arm so I figured it was true.

"Pollos."

"A pollero huh?" He looks at me incredulously. "Come on man. Pollero?"

"Yeah."

"Shouldn't mess with that homey no money in it. You should run drugs if you're gonna cross the border. That's where the big bucks is."

"Yeah, well I ain't even trippin homey. I'm just lookin to get out and go home. What about you ese? What they get you with?"

"Nothin."

"Yeah right, that's what they all say."

"No really. I'll tell you."

And so he did. And just when I thought I had heard all the fucked up shit I could hear about our government I learned one thing more. This poor guy. And I don't doubt what he says is true. As it happens he's going to see the same Judge as me, Judge Moskowitz. I got a year and the day from him as my sentence. Nice guy.

But Lomas, this guy was getting the royal shaft from our conservative and "compassionate" government. His name tells where he is from. Somewhere in California is a place called Lomas Hills or something like that and he's from there. Really. He was born there. After he was born his mother moved to Mexico when something went wrong with her and his father. Trouble was, she left and didn't bring his birth certificate with her. So when he was older he had to cross the border illegally. Even though he had a birth certificate at some county office the federal government didn't care and didn't give him a chance to get it when they deported him the first time and started his criminal record. The second time he got busted was for stealing cars. So yes, he actually did do something really bad at one point and served 6 years of his life in state prison for it. When he was released the Marshals picked him up and deported him. Again no chance to prove he was a citizen. This time, his fourth "illegal" entry, he was looking at 8 years, just because of his priors. He was hoping to finally change it all though by being allowed to present his birth certificate. Court procedures might not allow him to present that information at this time though.

The sad part was that he got caught this time just for being in the wrong place at the wrong time. The cops had come to bust another guy he just happened to be walking out of a house with. That guy got busted for grand theft auto and because he just happened to be with the guy and they found out he's illegal, they turned him over to the Marshals and he gets to do another eight year stretch.

No, granted, this guy was probably a pretty bad guy at one point, but eight years? That's $438,000 our government will spend on that one individual over the next eight years and after for his parole and probation. Meanwhile your baby or somebody's you know might not get adequate medical attention because they have no health insurance and the government says it doesn't have the resources to provide universal health care for everybody in this country. Or somebody else you may know just found out their student loan program was cancelled and they can't educate themselves anymore and instead have to work a grunt job for a company like Walmart or washing cars for some rich snob just to make ends meet and getting like a week old coffee cake as a tip from the skinflints at the carwash you work at. All because our government insists on spending huge sums of money to put people in jail for illegal entry into this country and for another war in Iraq that made our situation worse not better. I wonder what Ronald Reagan would have really said man. After all he was governor of California once and talked about how we needed to let these people in so our crops wouldn't rot on the vine. Heck, it was Reagan who refurbished the Statue of Liberty and Ellis Island back in July of 1986. (It was Reagan who asked " Are great numbers of our unemployed really victims of the alien invasion, or are those illegal tourists actually doing the work our own people won't do? One thing is certain in this hungry world: No regulation or law should be allowed if it results in crops rotting in the field for lack of harvesters." (see www.reagan.utexas. edu/archives/speeches.))

It was candidate Reagan who said "Some months before I declared, I asked for a meeting and crossed the border to meet with the president of Mexico. I did not go with a plan. I went, as I said in my announcement address, to ask him his ideas- how we could make the border something other than a locale for a nine foot wall." This was your president you right wing republican assholes. Your president. Did you listen to him? No. Instead over the years you made things worse by voting for progressively worse presidents. And our current president hasn't done a thing to create unity on this or any other issue. He hasn't tried to listen to anybody else's ideas. He's only concerned with the ones that come out of his intellectually challenged brain. As Hugo Chavez said recently in London, Bush is the number one terrorist in the world, a genocidal madman. He is the new Hitler of our time. And if we are not careful we will have worse than prisons pretty soon, we will have out and out concentration camps. Before it was the Jews in Germany and the Japanese here during WWII. Now it is the illegal Mexicans who are the unwanted portion of our society being picked on. Arabs too, just because we don't know if they are terrorists, but lets hold them anyway for years without even charging them with a crime. Soon its not going to be just Arabs or Mexicans, but anybody who does not agree with his viewpoint. Just like Hitler.

The Marshals come and start calling out names and men start to line up in the order they were called to get re-shackled before we go up into the courthouse. A little jostling here and there is usual for this scene. One guy in the corner is making strange gesticulations and sounds. He is obviously trying to prove he is insane so he can plead insanity as his defense. When you do that you must keep up that act all the time 24/7. So there he is building imaginary things and talking to imaginary people. What he's done nobody knows. And nobody cares. In here it is each man for himself. You can wheel and deal and make alliances but know one thing(from my perspective anyway); nobody is your friend in here. Nobody. The person that thinks he has a friend in here is a fool. Maybe for a moment somebody may be your friend, but not forever.

My name is called and I move to the line and wait. The Marshals open the gate and slowly we all go out. Down the hall in another cell are a group of women, mostly Latinas. Some have tattoos and you can tell they are gang bangers from one group or another. Like animals the men and women look at each other and think thoughts they know they will never get to fulfill. We are instructed not to talk or look at the women - at all. But some do. Those of us going to Moskowitz' courtroom go to a cell way down the hall and around the corner by an elevator. We're put in there and unshackled again. We wait some more.

Somewhere up above me inside the courthouse my attorney is waiting for me. Wow, how lucky I was to get him. See, in San Diego there are so many cases each year that the Public Defender's office can't handle all of them so the courts farm them out to attorneys in the community through a lottery system. I happened to get lucky by being given one of the top criminal defense attorneys in all of San Diego. He is quite a character. These long handle bars of a mustache grace his older face. He has grey hair and if it weren't for a suit and tie I could see him in a cowboy hat and boots in some other era. He is a true liberal. To hear him speak is to know that everything you ever suspected about the federal government is correct and that you can sleep at night knowing that you are not crazy or alone. If they want to call me a conspiracy theorist let them, because my attorney has in one way or another confirmed all my thoughts for me. Whether or not he is just acting doesn't matter either. Maybe he does that to all his clients. If he does I think its great. But I don't believe it is an act. He himself has acknowledged the failings of the very legal system he is a part of. He himself said we no longer live in a free country. He does what he can as one little individual attorney to stem the tide of the Holy Judicial Juggernaut sweeping over this country. And you know, some people get these other attorneys whose specialty isn't even criminal defense but real estate or insurance or some other type of law. Imagine getting a sports and entertainment lawyer as your criminal defense attorney! Thank goodness you are given three opportunities to fire your lawyer and get a new one before the judge tells you to stick with who you have because you're going to trial no matter what.

So I'm feeling good about this, even though my prosecutor is a total bitch named Jill Burkhart. Her nickname amongst even public defenders is Jill Blackheart. Of course it doesn't help matters any that her boss is Attorney General John Ashcroft. You all remember him right? He's the guy who couldn't defeat a dead guy in a Senatorial race in Missouri. So what happened? How did this guy become Attorney General? What secret deal with the devil did he make to get all the Democratic Senators (even Kennedy, who at first was against him, but then after a dinner with Bush at the White House was mum's the word about it) to confirm his nomination? We'll never know. But now he's suffering from prostate cancer. Even his shit is toxic to his own self. I think I'll make it a point to let the Blackheart know about how I feel about that one after all this is said and done.

Lomas and I are talking, and he asks again; "come on man,

what did you do? You're like a bilingual white guy. You had to be doin' something wrong man. You weren't no pollero man."

"Lomas, I said, "you really want to know my story?" I figured I'd never see Lomas again after this and he could tell just about anybody he wanted without any effect to me. My experience has been that when I start to tell people my story they know it is just too incredible to be a con. So I tell him all about it. And all he could do was sit there and listen;

"Lomas, I have been many things in this life so far. A son (sometimes not a good one), a grandson, a nephew and cousin. A brother and uncle. A student, a dishwasher, cook, and a prep cook. A high school grad, a college grad. World traveler, smuggler, protector of the poor. Basher of the rich. A Deadhead. A druggie, a drug dealer. A speaker salesman(selling them out of the back of a van in San Diego man), a wine salesman(in a wine shop, not out of the back of a van Come on man!). An amateur musician. A street musician. An express package delivery driver. A bumper sticker salesman. (Whispered)A marijuana grower. A marijuana seller. A waiter, a painter, a telephone canvasser, a door to door canvasser. A real estate agent. A lazy rich kid with nothing to do. A plaintiff and a defendant. A paralegal(supposedly). An English teacher, a Spanish teacher. A general laborer, a plumber, a mason, an interpreter and translator. A plasma donor. A Campfire counselor, A staff manager, a lead Spanish interpreter. A highly sought after candidate for the State department(I refused to even show up for the interview because I can't stand our government and the way it is conducting its business). A business owner with hundreds of people working for me. A homeless man. A chess player. A lover, a boyfriend a husband. A nanny! I have worked in wooden door factories. A landscaping maintenance guy and install. A farm hand. A counselor for homeless youth, homeless men and homeless Latino families. I have been a medical records clerk, an office manager in a mental health group home (wow and that was a real nutty one too homey.) A campaign organizer and a political candidate myself. I have been a yoga student and teacher."

He interrupted; "You're a yoga teacher?"

"Yep."

"Come on man. I don't buy that homey."

"Watch," I said as I proceeded to stand on my head and then go into the Scorpion posture right there in the waiting cell to go see the judge. The other inmates waiting to see Moskowitz all watched in silent amazement.

"Damn! Alright man." was all Lomas could say.

I sat down and continued on; " I have been a telephone researcher(how lame I know.) An adventure tour guide, a kitchen manager(twice). A hitchhiker(many times, I've hitchhiked all through Mexico, Central America(Panama, Costa Rica, Nicaragua, Honduras, El Salvador, Guatemala), the East coast of the United States and from Texas on west through California up to Portland, Oregon).

"I've been the victim of sexual harassment by three very large social workers," I said as I shuddered, "a camp counselor. Security for the Oregon Country Fair(if you know what that is.) A temp worker, a day laborer. A forest activist. A marijuana activist. A translator for the Zapatistas. An international peace observer(in Chiapas, Mexico, Queretaro Mexico and I had the pleasure of meeting Marcos and shaking his hand.) A customer service representative for Target.com. A brewery worker. An office worker for a mobile home manufacturer. A drywaller, a ditch digger, a front desk person for a gym(several actually) a breakfast cook, carpenter framer and finish carpenter. I have been unemployed and on food stamps and unemployment. I have been a writer and a poet. A vision quester. I have been both a good and a bad friend(who hasn't?) I have been a stock day trader. I have been a Socialist and an Independent but never a Democrat or Republican(I never did and never would give them my votes-ever). I've been an international street musician.

"I have been all those things and more homey. My father-in-law and my own parents would tell you I am a good for nothing lazy shiftless bum who can't hold a job for more than three months. But the truth of the matter is I am like so many other millions of Americans disenfranchised by this country. We are all called temp workers. The only difference between me and other temp workers who work through temp agencies is that instead of going through a temp agency and having them take two or three dollars off the top of my hourly slave wage, I keep that money by finding my own jobs homey. I also determine when my "temp assignment" is over by quitting a job when I want to instead of having the temp agency tell me when it ends. Long ago I stopped working for those temp agencies. They are just another useless middleman designed to cheat the American worker out of their hard earned money. Most mainstream people(my in-laws and parents included) wouldn't understand and would actually balk at the thought and call me a subvert or rebel. To them I say; who the hell cares what you think you represent less than 1% of the total population of not only this country but the world as well.

So after I have been all those things now I have been a human trafficker because I was too poor to get by and had no family there for me even though they could have been. A "pollero" man, a chicken driver. Soon I will be a prison inmate and when I get out a convicted felon on probation. How lovely."

He listened through all that. I could tell he understood and absorbed it all.

"I told you all that man because you are smart enough and

aware enough to understand it and see it too. Things as simple as all the inmates not showing up for work one day and forcing the feds to bring in outside people and pay them 12 dollars an hour to cook and clean instead of paying the inmates 12 cents an hour to do the same job. Then you'd see the B.O.P. figuring out how to do things a little more humanely. They'd be more respectful of basic human dignity. After all, just being locked up and denied your freedom and liberty is bad enough. No need to be cruel and unusual."

Again all he did was listen and nod. If there were microphones I didn't care. As a first timer I wouldn't be in too long and I just simply did not care. So I just unloaded the rest of my story on him just to blow his mind. If somebody was listening, good, let their minds be infected with my karmic adjustment.

"And hey man, what if all pre-trial inmates didn't take the deal? What if they didn't plead guilty to a lesser crime and sentence but demanded a trial instead? What if all of them did that and demanded a fast track as well You know what would happen homey? The courts would shut down and they would have to just start letting people go without a trial."

He just looked around as if he were afraid somebody was going to take us away for conspiracy against the system.

So, tell all them pre-trailers at Wackenhut to just demand a jury trial and to have their attorneys fast track them and sit back and see what happens!"

"Man," Lomas came back at me, "I grew up in Loma Linda Hills. To the man I am nothing more than a Mexican criminal. They'll fast track me alright, fast track me all the way to the Pen."

"Well I grew up in an upper class family in Cambridge, MA. So let them try to fast track me to the "Pen" for sticking up for my rights. I got a good education. Learned Spanish, a couple of instruments and when I graduated from college tried to live within the family fold. Unfortunately for various reasons that didn't work out. My parents were being too domineering for my taste and our parting was not amicable. That was many years ago in 1991 and I have not seen them since. They have not bothered to try and see their grandson or even send him a birthday card or Christmas card or anything of the kind. For my wedding my mom did send me something. In college I had cut my long hair off because my mother complained so much about it. I sent it to her in a box and when she got it she freaked out at first because she thought I had sent her a dead animal. Well, she is a nut, she saved that hair for seventeen years and sent it back to me as a wedding gift with a little note that read "I thought this would be an appropriate wedding gift for you...." How in the world anybody could think that was "appropriate" is beyond me."

From time to time life has been tough in these last sixteen years and I have been in need of assistance. My parents told me to go on food stamps because after all, they had paid enough taxes into the system, no reason one of their own family members shouldn't get some of it back in the way of food stamps. Can you believe that homey?"

"Homey, I been in prison a while and I learned a lot from reading all them books. I know them rich people well."

"Yeah well can you imagine this was the response to poverty coming from a multimillionaire who would rather see their kith and kin go hungry than lift a finger to help in a time of need. Even though I called them repeatedly to ask for help they refused me even though they very easily could have helped at no detriment to them. The issue is that they never forgave me for not going to law school when I got in and not only wouldn't help me after that but tried to hurt me more from time to time.

They claim to be Christians but I think they missed out on Jesus' main message of Love, Compassion, Forgiveness and responsibility. When I asked them (and my older brother who supposedly got a degree in philosophy) about their thoughts and viewpoints on these subjects they were non-responsive. Instead of responding to those queries they blathered on about other stuff, sidestepping the issues all together."

"Yeah, well I know about all them rich Christians too, homey. They come into the prisons with their missionaries thinking they are helping us. Telling us they're praying for us. One time I just straight up told them to save their prayers for themselves you know homey?" Lomas offered.

"I hear you homey. Those four words have come to make a really cool sentence in my mind homey. And I share it with as many of the rich snobs as I can. It goes like this; 'We have the responsibility to have love and compassion so we can forgive those who have wronged us.'

"Yeah man," was all Lomas said before I continued on.

"So check this out homey. My dad was a criminal defense attorney, he even carried around concealed handguns. I remember calls in the middle of the night and my dad going down to the police station to bail somebody out. But his own son? He not only didn't lift a finger to help me but while I was in prison he and my mother actually tried to get the trustees of my grandfather's testament and estate to make sure I couldn't have access to any information about the trusts. I am sure if they could have they would have disinherited me for going to prison. I think it angered he and my mom even more when the bank told them no and they couldn't accomplish that dastardly compassionless deed. Nowhere in my grandfather's will did it say 'and if you get busted and go to prison you get nothing from me.'

"Jealousy, greed and hate are destroying our lives on this

planet. You couldn't reduce the problems of this earth down to anything simpler than those three words homey."

I don't know what anybody else in the cell thought about what they heard. Who knew if they even understood English enough to fully comprehend. All Lomas did was nod. It was silent for a while once I had stopped.

One always looks back on their past to some degree when they are in jail. Especially when they are still waiting to be sentenced. It was kind of cool to be able to tell it all to a total stranger who was going away for a while and who I'd never see again.

Thus I found myself, one in 37 in this great country who goes to prison and one in 136 still in prison. What had I done? I wasn't a bad person. The Bible the prison gave me didn't mention anything about my "crime" as being bad. In fact some of those "good" people talked about in the bible actually had slaves and slept around and were still considered wise and ok. Yet here I was waiting to get out on bail. So I told Lomas the rest;

I told him how a whirlwind of forces had taken control of my life to land me in the Metropolitan Correction Center of San Diego, otherwise known as MCC. Thus its nickname: Mexican Country Club, MCC.

In the spring of 2003 I had lost my yoga center in Eugene, OR and my part time job ended because the company I worked for had closed its offices in Eugene, because they were no longer profitable there. Basically my job went to some other part of the country, or even worse, outsourced to some other country. My wife and I had just had a baby the year before and were expecting once again. We lived in our Yoga center in a house zoned residential/commercial. When we lost our business we went homeless.

I hadn't seen my family in years and my wife's family thought we were part of some cult like the Rajneeshi or something. With nobody to help, we were stuck in a real situation. Maybe if somebody had helped me get to Puerto Vallarta I wouldn't have been stuck in my situation. Nothing worse than feeling hopeless and not having any family standing by you when you most need it. What is family for anyway?

All we wanted was to move to Mexico and have our baby there. Since nobody would help me get there I had to do the only thing I could think of to get there on the limited funds I had available to me; hitchhike. My plan was to fly my wife and son down as soon as I was settled.

I have hitchhiked from Southern Costa Rica all the way through Central America and Mexico to Portland Oregon before, and on just $150. I had $275 this time and had only to reach Puerto Vallarta. But the journey north is much easier oddly enough from the journey south.

When I got to Tijuana I had only $200 left, a hundred of which I gave to a friend for safe keeping right before I got robbed and $25 of which I had spent on a hotel room for the night because I was just plum tired. I didn't get to see my friend again after I was robbed and I didn't know how to locate him so I was totally broke when these men approached me with their proposition. Being in the situation I was in I accepted. I figured even if I found my friend Esteban I could never make it to Puerto Vallarta and set up my life there on $100. So to make $600 a run across the Border seemed like a quick and easy solution to my problem. The consequences didn't matter because of the situation I was in. It didn't matter to me anymore because I had tried to lead a good life free of crime for many years and all it had gotten me was poor. During all that time all around me I saw the most tremendous corruption happening and people getting really rich by being really bad. So, tired of being poverty stricken because I was trying to do "good," I decided it was time I joined the ranks of the corrupt even if for a day, just so I could simply get by. Little did I know that my karma wouldn't permit even one day like that at this point in my life. I was no longer meant to do anything evil, corrupt or bad. And life was going to hard school me that lesson. Now I leave the evil doing and corruption to my government officials, corporations, their agents and those who support them.

If somebody had just helped me out, we could have gone to Puerto Vallarta and lived our dream life there and I could have avoided a bad mistake in the evil city of Tijuana. I would have easily found a job teaching English and we would have lived happily ever after. But no. Jealousy and hatred conspired against me. My karma had to take me to rock bottom. I had to gain a greater understanding of what millions of others already know. Our government and our society is based on profit. When you are down and out they let you stay there. Someone is making a living off of your desperation. Yeah, there may be truly helpful groups out there, but the majority are helping themselves make a profit, not you. Without troublemakers and losers to take care of they would be out of a job. We can only be responsible for our own actions The Word says "Love thy neighbor as thyself." Regardless of my trouble I needed somebody to be there for me. What I learned is that this society doesn't want to be there for you unless it stands to gain something from being there for you. Money has to be made from the downtrodden! Just think about all those Christians, they aren't following Jesus' words at all.

You never know the value of a person until they are tested by the worst of situations I thought. And this thought, "if somebody had just helped me....." is repeated day after day in our nation's courts. How many people who go to prison wouldn't be there if their family or other support networks hadn't failed them? When somebody is down they need help, not another kick in the teeth. Wasn't this Jesus' message somewhere in the Good Book too?

We compared notes about the differences between MCC and Wackenhut. Seems as a privately run prison facility Wackenhut is able to provide different things for its inmates. Longer TV. hours. Better prison store items (although I don't know what that really meant.) More time outside for recreation (MCC lets you out only once a week, Wackenhut lets you out once a day for one hour.) We also talk about the Border and the trouble it is causing our countries.

"You know," I tell him, "what all the Mexicans should do is not cross. The ones already here should go back for just three months, heck just three weeks and they'll have the U.S.A. on its knees begging them to come back. With nobody to pick the crops, serve the fast food, do the construction, clean the houses and offices this country would suffer. At the same time the Mexican government should just legalize marijuana. If its legal a whole new economy opens up which provides work for all those unemployed and they won't need to go north for work. From cultivating to harvesting to transportation and sales. Mexico can let the world know in its tourism ads that, hey, come to Mexico, smoke and not get hassled by cops. Tranquilo like in Amsterdam. You know how many people would go to Mexico and never come back because of that homey?"

"You're right homey. It would be glorious to see the change happen. Maybe some day," is all Lomas has to offer. These are taboo subjects for people still awaiting sentencing and possibly being listened to here in the holding cell. Later I'll find out how the Blackheart uses my political views to discriminate against me and argue for a longer than usual prison sentence for me. Oh well. I feel like Ricardo Flores Magon. If you don't know who he is you should really find out more about him. Our government wrongfully persecuted him and put him in prison many times simply for trying to run a newspaper in L.A. They raided his printing presses and destroyed them many times over the years during the 20's and 30's. He died in prison an innocent man. So what our government is doing now isn't anything new. We claim to have a free press and media, only as long as the media agrees with the administration. If not, look out, the thought police will find a way to jail you to get you out of their hair. With 90 percent of the media controlled by less than a hundred different families its easy for the government to have them all on a list with phone numbers and everything so that if they don't report the news the way the government wants them to they can be called and secretly threatened to report it "right" or else.

Immigration issues aren't new to the media or the country. This problem has been happening for at least a century. First it was those evil Southern Europeans and Jews. So they made a law about restricting immigration from those countries and those types of people. Actually it was the immigration quota against Jewish immigration which is partly to blame for the Holocaust being able to happen in such grand fashion in the first place. Kind of funny how now we will do anything to make sure they are o.k. as if it were out of our own collective and subconscious national guilt complex. But the truth of the matter is we give more foreign aid money to Israel than any other country in the world.

The guards come and call out Moskowitz' docket and we move to the door. This time we are not all shackled together but before we get on the elevator we get patted down again, then onto the elevator and up to the fifth floor. We get out and are taken to a really small holding cell with a toilet and sink. While we wait I stand on my head for five minutes. A guard comes and scurries off not sure if he's supposed to let me do that. The other inmates laugh. Its amazing how a guard can feel threatened by a man standing on his head. We wait for what seems like forever and then luckily I am called out first. I guess because my name starts with A. I am escorted into the courtroom after one last pat down. There is my attorney and Ms. Blackheart.

My attorney goes through the bail agreement with the judge and he asks the prosecutor if she agrees. Of course she does since it was her evil hearted idea anyway. Basically since nobody would sign for my bail the agreement is to allow my wife and I to sign for my own bail. In exchange I have had to agree to give up any right to argue for a "downward departure" when it comes to my sentencing hearing. Basically Blackheart here just cost the taxpayers more money than they needed to pay for my punishment. About $36,450 more. If I could have argued for downward departures I probably would have done like three months at the most. But without downward departures I am looking at a year to 18 months, possibly even three years.

All the court formalities are done and my bail has been approved. I look around the courtroom and for the first time notice that nobody is in there but the lawyers, the judge, the Marshals and I. I whisper to my attorney about it and he tells me that they had cleared the courtroom before I entered and that they usually do that when they don't want the general public to know what is going on. How strange. What were they afraid of? What did they think I would do or say? Now I really feel like Ricardo Flores Magon. And I have his same first name. Maybe I was him in my last life. Except this time I am a pollero trying to run his people across the border and into this country.

So I am public enemy number one. So dangerous they needed to clear the courtroom so nobody would be infected with my politics. Wow. Whatever. As I am escorted out Mark and I exchange smiles. In a matter of hours I will be out and on the streets with a Greyhound bus ticket to Oregon waiting for me.

I am taken back to the holding cell. And have to wait as one by one the others go before the judge. As they come back I ask them if the courtroom was empty or not. Full. Packed with family members and other interested members from the public. Wow. I feel special. As soon as we are all done we are taken back down into the basement of the courthouse where we wait to be transferred back to MCC or Wackenhut. While we wait, since we missed lunch back in the unit, we are given sack lunches. These lunches consist of one sour apple and three white bread sandwiches with a singe slice of bologna or cheese stuck in the middle. What I call the 10 cent lunch.

We're telling jokes as we wait. So I tell a couple to Lomas to take back to Wackenhut with him.

"Hey Lomas," I say, " sixty percent of all men masturbate in the shower, the other forty percent sing a special song they know, you know what it is?"

"No what homey?"

"I didn't think so." It takes a while for it to register and then he laughs real hard and says "yeah homey, I ain't goin to lie, I been in prison most of my adult life so yeah I masturbate in the shower." In fact so many men do that they sell shower shoes at the prison store. And especially at MCC you need them, not just cause of the sperm floating around on the floor, but because of the green worms that come crawling up out of the drain to eat it. At one point during my two month vacation at MCC Curly asked me if I masturbated. When I told him no he freaked.

"Man, that is what is wrong with you. You need to jerk off man or you'll go crazy up in this fucker. Straight up man, go right now and jerk off, you'll see how much better you feel afterwards." I just laughed. I couldn't tell a man like him that it was actually the other way around, that if you masturbate it leads to general agitation and anger. He wouldn't get it.

Then I told another joke. This time I had them all laughing. This joke was a joke that a Mexican trucker told me once when I hitched a ride from Tepic, Nayarit to Nogales Arizona.

"How come there are no Mexicans in the Olympics?" I say.

"I don't know homey why?" asked Lomas.

"Because all the Mexicans who can run, jump or swim have already crossed the border." Man what an uproar, so much so that a Marshal had to come and see what was going on even though we are all being watched on closed circuit television. If you can laugh in prison, that's when the time passes by a little faster it seems. If you're just going to sit around and blubber your head off then forget it. That's called "hard timing it." And nobody wants that. So if you are going to hard time it save it for the middle of the night and cry softly into your pillow or something so nobody hears or sees it. Its already hard enough without that shit going on.

Finally the Marshals get it together and come for us. Shackled and patted down for the umpteenth time we are finally on our way back through the underground corridor. When we get to the door leading into MCC we are all asked our names and numbers and checked off.

Once back in the unit I go straight to my bunk and start rolling it up. I am out of here. Curly and Chicharron, now the shot callers for Whites and Mexicans respectively, come up to me. They ask me how it went.

"Good man. I have some good news for you boys. Jay-Lo is already in the hospital. They fucked him up the other day because they all found out he was a snitch for something else he did to them or some shit like that." You should have seen these two men's happiness. Like school children. Like I said some of these people deserve to be here, no denying that. We just need a better justice system that can determine who really needs to be in prison and who doesn't. And we do not need to be spending 50 billion a year to incarcerate illegal aliens. What a total waste. 50 billion spent on the border could keep them out forever if that was what our government really wanted to do. But it doesn't.

So they are happy. I'm happy I'm out of here. As I pack my things they ask me for some of my stuff. Nail clippers, whatever. Extra sheets, socks, shampoo, soups or food. I divide it all up and give it to them. They will find out who amongst their groups needs those things and give them to them. That is how it works. If you think our society is political, prison is even more so, except there is no democracy in there. Straight up oligarchies, rule by the strongest. I tried to mitigate that while I was there. I used to give my extra food to the smallest guy in there, not the biggest. In the process I pissed some people off. But they finally figured out that they couldn't get me to follow along in the pre-trial unit. One Paisa told me "just you wait homey until you get to the real pen, then you'll be doin' what we tell you to."

"Until then homey, I'll do what I want," I said. I even had a guard tell me that after I talked smack to him for being a dipshit to me. "You wouldn't be treating me like that at a USP (United States Penitentiary)," he said.

"No I wouldn't," I retorted, "but then again we're not at a USP so suck it up." That was my second to last day there when I was pissed because we hadn't had any air conditioning for the last forty-eight hours and some of the inmates were starting to get light headed for lack of oxygen. It was a major emergency because the prison had to lock us all down for a while and open all the doors leading to the various floors all the way down to the main entrance door and let fresh air trickle in that way just so we wouldn't all suffocate to death. Somebody said its because MCC didn't have enough money to pay its electric bill. We all laughed. Later it was discovered a rat(literally) had gotten in to one of the primary a.c. units and triggered a shutdown of some sort and repair men had to come fix the damn thing. Leave it to rats to screw things up for you.

Curly and Chicharron said their goodbyes. They were happy. They had there revenge and some new stuff. Pops started to cry because I was going. "I wish you weren't going," he said.

"That's not a nice thing to wish Pops," said Indio with a smile.

"I know, but his being here has made it easier for the rest of us and now when he's gone I'm afraid they'll put us all on different floors and I won't have anybody there for me anymore."

"I'll always be there for you pops. When you get out just come find me and I'll look after you as you get older pops. I wouldn't do that for my own pops, so I might as well do it for you to make up for it. And don't worry there will always be somebody there for you here on the inside Pops." I felt bad for him. I didn't want to tell him what I really saw. Always try to uplift the downtrodden. Never try to kick them while they are down. That's the lesson my father-in-law is learning right now as you read these words.

My bunkie John was waiting to talk with me. I had already secretly given him the best of my stuff that I didn't need and he was very thankful. Poor guy. To this day, three years later he is still awaiting trial without bail. I will never forgive this government's cruelty even though I know I am supposed to forgive and forget, something I learned from my yoga teachings. Maybe someday.

"Brother, I have a hundred dollars waiting for you when

you walk out of here today." He always said things like that. He was always saying to the prayer group that all their stories would be heard in the book he was writing. Once he got out he would publish it and use the proceeds to help others throughout the world. That is why I am writing it, because he may never get the chance to and it can't wait any longer. There is no need for any more suffering than has already been going on in this world, especially the suffering going on in the name of Jesus. All those Christians calling for war need to remember Jesus didn't say "when your enemy strikes you go bomb the heck out of them." He said "turn the other cheek." So turn the other cheek! And I am not talking about your overweight fat assed butt cheeks either. I'm talking about following the true spirit of his message. He said to turn the other cheek so you could minimize the impact of negative karma on your life. If you strike back you just prolong and perpetuate bad karma. By not reacting, but turning the other cheek you lessen your own negative karma. Don't get me wrong I am not a church going Bible thumping Christian. Just somebody who believes that a very special man named Jesus had a very special message for us all.

"How do you have a hundred dollars waiting for me?" I asked. I didn't believe him but I always liked to see what people had to say. And John liked to make those kinds of promises.

"You'll see. Its at the Greyhound station waiting for you. Don't disbelieve the word of a spiritual warrior my brother."

"Ok I won't Brother John." I just figured it was the words of an old man who wished he had more "juice" than he actually did. But whatever. I continued to ready myself. Took my last piss. Made my last rounds to say goodbye to that handful of people who knew I was leaving.

By now everybody could see I was leaving though. After

all, all my stuff was rolled up and waiting to go. I went to say goodbye to Octavo. He was so happy to see me go. He was almost out of here himself. In a couple of days after I left his trial would happen and he would be declared innocent and he'd be back in Tijuana seeking revenge himself and in the process he'd turn into one of the biggest crime bosses of Tijuana. See, if you kill the top guy and you yourself have buckets of cash to fling around then you become numero uno. That's what eventually became of him, but that is a separate story for another book.

"Hey man, I hope you get out of here soon." I said.

"I will homey. And I don't ever want to see you back in here yourself. I don't even want to here of it. Your wife and kids need you back up in Oregon. So don't screw it up for yourself Alevizos or I'll kick your ass. Now get the hell out of my sight!"

"Ok Octavo." We hugged and exchanged phone numbers. I thought I would never hear from him again, but I did several times before he dropped off the face of the earth again. Who knows maybe back in prison with an alias or living underground in Tijuana.

This little Mexican came up to me, they called him Chapo, or "shorty" in English. He was seriously like 4 foot 6, borderline midget. He was the one I always gave my extra food to. He hugged me too with a tear in his eye. He was a hard knocks case. He was from Chiapas and had no money or relatives to call because they didn't have a phone where he lived. So he was truly all alone right now in the world. Being from Chiapas he was used to a much higher quantity of fruit intake in his diet and so I always made sure to give him some of my fruit. I never kept it for myself. If I couldn't get it to him for some reason like a lock down situation then I gave it to the old or sick. Part of my selfless service to the poor lost souls of MCC San Diego. I know in prison you are supposed to suffer. But they are not supposed to be subtly killing you off through lack of nutrition.

"Hasta Luego Chapo," I never knew his real name, first or last and it never mattered in a place like this.

"Hasta luego gavacho." And he was gone.

Then came the call for the afternoon count. A little early it seemed. It was only three fifteen in the afternoon and the count wasn't supposed to happen until four. Back in the range a couple of Mexicans came up to me. Don Chewy was one of them. He had a whole gaggle of kids at home. I could tell he wished he was me. They all did. Not a man in there didn't wish he was hitting the streets like me.

Topos, came up to me and thanked me for showing him how to do a headstand. They called him Topos because he was from a place called Topolobampo.

One of the Columbians, Changaro, who I had helped came up to me and thanked me again for helping get him a lighter sentence than what he would have gotten. They called him Changaro, or monkey, because he seriously had some big floppy ears. If he had made it across the border all that cocaine he could have sold could have gotten him a good cosmetic surgery like any rich person in Beverly Hills. I'd wager he was more deserving of it too.

Felix came up to me then and hugged me. He didn't say anything. His lower lip was quivering. He was too young to be going to a maximum security for six years. All because of two kilos of cocaine.

I smiled at him.

"Ahora, que no te metes con putos asi no agarraras piojos cavron. Don't get involved with gay hookers and you won't get crabs fucker." He laughed then and his face became brighter.

For the first time, now that I was really leaving, I could see the true desperation on the faces of these men. In some way or another I had helped them all. Either through yoga or translating or teaching English. Or just being there to listen to them vent about their cases. Or standing up to the in-humaneness of the guards(and not getting taken away to the hole for doing so.) Or making them laugh at my jokes.

My name was called out and as I walked out and sat in the main central area with one other man who also was getting out today all the other inmates came to the gates of their various ranges and started shouting our names and goodbyes to us. I could see all their faces as if from afar. A collage of desperation.

Some were just totally silent. Felix, the young cocaine trafficker who had had crabs and had become my friend, was standing there staring at me with a sad smile on his face. I knew what was going through his mind. He knew his day wasn't going to be for a long time and he wished it was different. At one point I had told him to cheer up. Maybe he'd only get three years instead of six.

John was there holding up his hand to me like Jesus did with two fingers tucked into the palm. He was mouthing the words "You'll see." A tear trickled down his face too. He must have known the long hard road ahead of him which he takes to this day.

All four ranges were full of men looking at us, mostly at me. I gave them all my loudest Mexican war cry "Aaaaaah Haaaaa Aiiiiiiii," and said "Hijos de la Malinche!" and they all resounded with a resounding "HILO CAVRON." and they kept saying it until the guards came and took us out into the elevator corridor. I was lucky the prison officials didn't want to charge me with trying to incite a prison riot.

The door to the unit shut and that part of my life was now behind me. We stood quietly waiting for the elevator. Me, the guards and one other Mexican dude getting out on bail.

The elevator door opened and there of all people stood officer Butridge.

"Ritchie of Oz. So they're letting you out." You could tell he was pissed.

"Yep, looks like your prison sentence is longer than mine there pal."

"Don't worry," he said, "you'll be back."

"Not a chance. But you'll be stuck here for years to come. And at eight hours a day you'll spend almost a third of your life in prison while I'm on the outside laughing at you and your tiny salary," I said real quiet like.

"We'll see Mexican lover." He was trying his hardest to say anything he could to piss me off. But he couldn't. He was ignorant and all I could do was be thankful I wasn't.

We got to the second floor where they put me in a cell to wait for my property. The cell had been freshly painted. it's a good thing I had a pen on me. So many people left graffiti on the walls of these cells they had to periodically paint them. With this clean wall I did miracles. I left my handle on all the walls so when the other inmates would come down from the seventh floor in the next week or two they would all remember me and laugh. That way even after I was gone I would be a bright spot in their day.

The release part was somewhat interesting. It's like these BOP prison guards and their captains don't want to let you go. Your job security to them. If the prisons empty then they go on unemployment. So they really hate to see you go. And they drag the whole process out as much as possible. Asking for your social security number after every step of the process and your prison i.d. number. So I'd give it to them, but in super slo mo as if they were the stupidest beings on the planet. Each time they made me repeat these numbers you could tell the mounting frustration as I held them all up. Until finally one of them said to me "We'll see you back here again asshole and then you'll really pay."

"I don't think so. But dream on."

They finally escorted me to the first floor of MCC. I walked out into a cool October afternoon. My first instinct was to look up and see if I could tell which floor was the seventh and if anybody was looking down on me. Then I started walking and didn't look back. And I didn't see MCC again until I went back down t San Diego for my sentencing hearing the next spring.

I walked two blocks to the Greyhound station and picked up my ticket. To my surprise I found a hundred dollars waiting for me.

"Bless his soul," was all I could say. Then something strange happened. A man came up to me and identified himself as a person who knew the people I was driving the lady across the border for.

"What do you want man?" I asked.

"Hey come to Tijuana they have another job for you so you can make some big money."

"If you got the money up front right now homey." I knew he didn't I was just teasing.

"No homey, don't have no money on me right now."

"Tell them to western union it to me then homey."

"OK," he said as if they really would and walked away. They never did contact me again. It was like a brush with temptation. A karmic test. This time I had passed and got on that bus.

After a 24 hour bus ride to Eugene and a three and a half hour car ride with a person who claimed to be my friend but later proved otherwise, I finally made it to Bend, Oregon. My plan was to make it back in time for the birth of my second son. I had been there for the first and caught him myself.

This time I wasn't so fortunate. I had arrived two hours late. My wife birthed our son at home in the water. She spent 31/2 hours in hard labor. She spent the majority of it crying, she wouldn't let her midwife let go of her hand. With her tears she released our suffering from going homeless, losing a business, and my crossing the border. I made a mistake, While I was down and out I made a choice and I paid for it. And my family paid for it too.

What about the people from Mexico and other countries who are crossing the border to fulfill their dreams in the land of opportunity? What about their families? Since when is it a land of opportunity only for some? These people are needed here. Without them jobs necessary for the survival of our country would not get done. Do we need to eat fruits and vegetables? Do you like to have a fast-food meal every now and then? With the focus on the borders we are avoiding our real issues; the education system, corporate accountability, healthcare, the environment. Unfortunately our society is good at avoiding. And denying and deflecting. it's the new definition I've given to the term ADD. Avoid deflect and deny. And in extreme cases add an "ID" at the end to make ADDID; Avoid, Deflect, Deny, and if need be Invalidate and then Destroy if that doesn't work. Its just the fascist way is what I say. Instead of this "me" generation neo fascism;

Let us love our neighbors as ourselves. It's time to let go of the idea that we need to be in control of material resources and have dominion over others. We need to be focusing on providing basic needs to all instead. We need to be fighting the crimes of greed. We the people, the poverty stricken population of the earth need to rise up and safeguard mankind's survival. Let our prisons be filled with those who take more than they need, and give little in return. Not with those that are barely getting by striving to survive.

POSTSCRIPT

I found this years ago and made a couple of changes. No author has come forward and it has been anonymously donated.

Anote of appreciation from the rich;

Lets be real: You'll probably never win the lotto. On the other hand, chances are pretty good that you'll slave way the rest of your life at some miserable job the majority of your life. That's because you were in all likelihood born into the wrong economic group. Sorry!

Because of this, you don't have the education, upbringing, connections, manners, appearance and good taste to ever become a rich socialite. In fact, you'd need a book the size of the yellow pages to list all the unfair advantages that rich socialites have over you. That is why the rich are so relieved to know that you still believe all those silly fairy tales about "justice" and "equal opportunity" in America.

In a hierarchical social system like ours there has never been much room at the top. So sorry. And its already occupied by the rich socialites and they like it so much that they intend to stay there.

But at least there is always someone lower in the social hierarchy you can feel superior to and kick in the teeth once in a while. Even a lowly dishwasher can easily find someone else lower down in the pecking order to sneer and spit at. So be thankful for migrant workers, prostitutes and the homeless.

Always remember that if everyone like you were economically secure and socially privileged like us, there would be no one left to fill all those boring, dangerous, low paid jobs in our economy. And no one to fight our wars for us, or blindly follow orders in our totalitarian corporate institutions And certainly no one to meekly go to their grave without having lived a full and creative life. So please, keep up the good work!

You also probably don't have the same greedy compulsive drive to possess wealth, power and prestige like the rich socialites. And even though you may sincerely want to change the way you live, you are afraid of the very change you desire. So you go through life playing your assigned role, terrified what others might think should you dare break out of the "mold."

Naturally, the rich try to play you off against each other when it suits their needs: high wage workers against low waged, unionized against non-unionized, Black against White, male against female, American workers against Japanese against Mexican and so on and so on. The rich continually push your wages down by invoking "Foreign competition", "the law of supply and demand," "national security," or the poor "bloated federal deficit." If you don't watch out those rich will throw you on the unemployed scrap heap for stepping out of line or jeopardizing corporate profits.

As if it were a break from the monotony of the daily economic blackmail we go through the rich allow us to participate in their stage managed electoral shell games better known to us common folk as "elections." Happily you don't have a clue as to what is really happening- instead you blame aliens, the illegal ones too, "Tree huggers," "Niggers," "Jew," "Welfare Queens," and countless others for your situation.

The rich are quite pleased that many of us still embrace the "work ethic," even though most jobs in our economy degrade the environment, undermine your physical and emotional health, and basically suck your one and only life right out of you. The rich don't know much about work, but they are sure glad you do.

Life could be different, Society could be intelligently organized to meet the real needs of the general population. You and others like you could collectively fight to free yourselves from Rich domination. But most people would never think of that. It is beyond their imagination that another way could exist. And that is probably the single greatest achievement of the rich socialite system- robbing you of your imagination, your creativity and your ability to think for yourself.

So from the bottom of their heartless hearts the rich would truly like to thank you. Your loyal sacrifice makes possible their corrupt luxury; your work makes their system work and they are right now somewhere on their yachts thanking you for "knowing your place" even without knowing it.